# MAKING
# GAY RELATIONSHIPS
# WORK

**Terry Sanderson**

The Other Way Press

For Keith, who helps me practise what I preach.

**The Other Way Press**

Published by The Other Way Press, PO Box 130, London W5 1DQ.
1994. 2nd edition.

Acknowledgements: Bruce Hugman, John Lyttle, The Independent.

Cover design by Number 20 Design Consultants. Tel: 0905 -57823
Printed by Bailes Fastprint, Houghton-le-Spring, DH5 8AN

Other books by Terry Sanderson
How to be a Happy Homosexual (GMP Publishers)
Assertively Gay: How to build gay self-esteem
A Stranger in the Family: How to cope if your child is gay
The Potts Correspondence and other gay humour
From bookshops or by mail from The Other Way Press, PO Box 130,
London W5 1DQ (send s.a.e. for more details).

# *Contents*

Introduction .................................... 1

1. Glad to be gay? ........................... 15
2. How do gay couples meet? ............. 53
3. When to take the plunge ................ 68
4. The ground rules ........................ 93
5. Ringing the changes ................... 105
6. Other people's approval .............. 128
7. Relationship skills .................... 145
8. Jealousy ................................ 160
9. Sex ..................................... 179
10. The end of the road ................... 214

Epilogue ................................... 241

Listings .................................... 248

# INTRODUCTION

According to official statistics, there were 436,346 marriages registered in the UK in 1974; by 1990 the figure had dropped to 375,410. Currently the number is falling by 7 per cent a year. Divorce rose from 25,000 in 1961 to 153,386 in 1990. Numbers are still rising and almost half of all marriages now end in divorce.

It would appear from these figures that marriage for heterosexuals is going out of fashion. And yet, within ten days of gay marriages (or, more accurately, 'partnerships') being legalised in Denmark in October, 1989, 400 gay couples had come forward to register their relationships and see them attain official (if not universal) blessing. Now other Scandinavian countries have followed suit and several other European nations are considering similar legislation. There are literally thousands of registered gay couples now.

In Britain, of course, gay partnerships are mentioned only once in law (as the "pretend family relationships" of section 28). But even that calculated insult cannot stop the debate about recognising and even legalising partnerships between members of the same sex.

## *Making Gay Relationships Work*

Significantly, a report commissioned by the Church of England, and leaked to the press in 1990, had acknowledged that the issue of gay partnerships could not be ignored. The report, chaired by the Reverend June Osborne, asked the Church to consider the question of "services of blessing for same sex couples". It stated: "What is clear is the need for the Church to affirm the value of same sex friendships and consider ways in which support and structures can be provided to enable those friendships to flourish."

Pretty radical stuff for an institution as deeply conservative as the Anglican church, and an indication that at least the issue is up for discussion, even if it may be decades away from a conclusion.

But while worthy members of the Establishment wring their hands over whether they can "accept" gay partnerships, those individuals who are gay and in love have set about the business of actually forming their relationships and making them work—most of us do not feel the need to wait for the permission of "the authorities" before we make a start. We know that the approval of the law would, perhaps, relieve a little of the burden upon us, but we also know that some of the hardest problems will come from the difficulties of actually finding a partner and then making a relationship with him work.

Most gay couples are well aware of the extra difficulties facing them in their life together, including the greater chance of hostility from family and friends. And yet still we try. If, like the rest of the human race, we want to love and be loved, we have little choice but to take the risks.

This book will look at some of the pressures that gay couples face, from inside and outside their relationship. It will hopefully help identify and neutralise some of the pitfalls into which the unwary can fall. We can, as we set out on our own journey of discovery, learn from the mistakes of our brave predecessors. Their efforts and experiences have provided researchers with a great deal of information about the structures and dynamics of gay relationships. Some progress has been made in identifying precisely what it is (besides the obvious) that makes a gay relationship different from a straight one. If we are aware of these findings they can help us immeasurably when we encounter the inevitable turbulent times with our own partners.

## Is It Worth The Hassle?

In the past, activists in the sexual liberation movements have argued that pair-bonding is merely a means of control, invented in order to make society more manageable. In 1971 the Gay Liberation Front published a leaflet which said: "We do not deny that it is possible for gay couples as for some straight couples to live happily and constructively together. We question however as an ideal the family and settling down eternally with one right partner. This is the blueprint of the straight world which gay people have taken over."

Human beings—go these arguments—aren't naturally monogamous, and the high incidence of infidelity among married men and women is cited as proof. It is even said in support of the argument that in the animal world only a tiny handful of creatures— including the wolf and the trumpeter swan—are monogamous. But, as many gay couples know, monogamy is not absolutely essential in order to give a relationship the "committed" status. It's a matter of personal choice and personal needs.

3

Still, it was argued, having one partner for life—or large sections of our life—seems to be the phoney ideal imposed on us by religious and political institutions because it helps them perpetuate their own power. The obsession by authoritarian religionists about "family values" and "traditional models", seems to support this. The same reasoning says that a huge conditioning process has taken place over the centuries to brainwash us into the idea that a committed relationship is the only sensible way to live - anything less is 'immature'.

In its heyday, Hollywood used its undoubted influence to project the ideal of romantic and exclusive love as the only sure way to happiness. Almost every major film made during the thirties, forties and fifties seemed to say that marriage was 'normal' and anything else beyond the pale. Adulterers, good time girls and homosexuals were almost inevitably doomed before the end of the final reel. The unquestioned assumption that there is only one acceptable way to live was pushed relentlessly. Nowadays newspapers and advertising fulfil the same role of pushing marriage as the 'natural' unit of society.

Such a restricted view of the world has created a great deal of unhappiness for people who can't, won't or don't want to tow the conventional line. Thankfully, the oppressive nature of this idea is being challenged, particularly by women who are fed up with having their lives pre-ordained by the conventions created by someone else, and society is becoming a little more flexible in its outlook.

Even so, the majority of people continue to harbour the dream of an on-going (if not monogamous) primary relationship. Even if they don't believe in one-to-one for ever, they might believe in one-to-one at a time (or serial monogamy).

The previously quoted divorce statistics seem to show that vast numbers of heterosexuals aren't particularly good at making their relationships last. It's not clear whether this is because they lack the necessary relationship skills or because they have unrealistic expectations in the first place. Maybe it is simply that the whole institution of marriage is artificial and inevitably doomed to failure. Many of the marriages that do survive are regarded by the participants as some kind of penance rather than a joy; the popular music hall image of marriage is of a millstone around a man's neck, and a prison for the woman. Relatively few straight couples are able to state, with hand on heart, that their relationship has provided them with the level of fulfilment they had hoped for.

So, let's get away from the idea that gay relationships, because of their very nature, can't work. This idea is propounded by conventional heterosexuals who disregard the fact that straight relationships don't work much of the time either. Relationships—straight or gay—*can* work, if those involved are prepared to nurture them.

## The Gay Emergence

After Gay Liberation arrived in the early seventies, people whose sexual attraction was mainly towards members of their own sex felt confident enough to try and make a lifestyle out of it. Of course, others had tried before, but severe legal and social sanctions made fully functioning relationships very difficult to sustain. As these pressures lessened, and people became more open and less afraid, exploration began. The early pioneers went in two directions: some tried to ape marriage, setting up home together with a division of roles very much like a man and wife; others rejected all the heterosexual trappings inventing a completely new way of living. The gay lifestyle was born. Many felt that their sexuality 'liberated' them from the need to pair-bond. They felt no need to make commitments which they regarded as artificial, and much of the gay scene consisted of a sexual merry-go-round that was exciting and dangerous. New possibilities were explored - for example communal living which did not recognise private property or monogamy or jealousy. Some tried it, but few succeeded over an extended period.

Some men had a primary relationship in which each partner gave the other the freedom to enjoy as many other sexual partners as he desired. Many simply made no ongoing commitments, taking their pleasures as and when they wanted, with no reference to anyone else. Casual or 'recreational' sex became the norm in the gay community. Why should it not? There seemed no need to impose controls on pleasant, and sometimes pressing, natural urges; if men are sexual beings, and both partners are willing, why should they hold back? Most gay relationships would have no children attached to them, so there was no need to pair-bond for the purposes of child-rearing.

And yet even at the height of such freedom there were those who felt the need for something else. The unending licence seemed, for some men, like a straitjacket: there could be no rest from the hunt, no respite from the excitement. The need for a deeper and more stable kind of love seemed to be asserting itself even before the arrival of Aids. The American playwright Harvey Fierstein put his finger on it when he said: "Gay liberation should not be a license to be a perpetual adolescent. If you deny commitment, then what can you do with your life?"

Dr. Bernard Zilbergeld put it this way:

"The only important question you need to answer is whether impersonal sex works for you. If you are satisfied, fine. We know, however, that many men are not happy with it. They do it but they are not content and wish for something better. The human contact it provides is illusory and the sexual release it affords is often less satisfying than what could have been derived from masturbation."

## The HIV Factor

So much has been written about Acquired Immune Deficiency Syndrome and the whys and wherefores of its spread among homosexuals, that we need not repeat it here. A period of deep shock settled over the gay community as the likely consequences of the virus became clear. That shock is lessening, but those who are left are now looking for new ways to order their lives.

Safer sex is, of course, a means of minimising the risk of infection, but safer sex doesn't seem enough. Aids has made us, as gay men, look more carefully at the way we are living - it has made us realise that perhaps there are avenues of love that we have not yet adequately explored and which will render rewards for those who will try.

Many gay men are becoming amenable to the idea of "settling down" and trying to make it work. Indeed, the Kinsey Institute in America published the findings of Alan Bell and Martin Weinberg who interviewed 686 gay men in California and found that 51 per cent were currently involved in a steady relationship. Their detailed analysis of the lives of these men concluded: "Our data tends to belie the notion that homosexual affairs are apt to be inferior imitations of heterosexual premarital or marital involvements."

## Challenging The Myths

Straight men and women who don't have husbands or live-in partners are often regarded as failures. A special place is reserved in the heterosexual hierarchy for "spinsters" and "confirmed bachelors". The contempt in such terms is apparent. Gay relationships, on the other hand, have been traditionally scorned by society and the resultant pressures have made them difficult to sustain. But, as we've said, that is being challenged. The journalist Brenda Maddox has written about these ambivalent attitudes to homosexual relationships in a *Sunday Telegraph* article:

"The advance of Aids, a disease which in the United States has spread first and fastest amongst homosexuals, has increased the public's awareness and dislike of homosexual promiscuity. Homosexuals are being urged to stick to stable relationships. Is it not, therefore, hypocritical and even dangerous to castigate a large section of the population for undesirable behaviour, while withholding the remedy most likely to discourage such behaviour?"

Ms Maddox is firmly of the opinion that it should be possible for gay men to make legally recognised relationships with each other. But before this can happen we need to change not only the ingrained attitudes of society, but also the deeply-rooted negative ideas that have been internalised by gay people themselves. So many men limit themselves because they have accepted the myths that 'gay relationships don't last' or that two men can't successfully live together as a couple because neither would be prepared to be 'the woman'. We have also been told that because gay couples don't produce children, their partnerings are 'sterile'; or because such a relationship is 'abnormal' it cannot be sustained. Even some supposedly liberal heterosexuals will tell you that if both partners are of the same sex there is an imbalance—a lack of yin and yang—and so the relationship is inferior. However, if we look at these ideas objectively, we will see that they are nonsense.

## The Butch-Femme Myth Laid to Rest

Research - and our own observations - have proved that the "butch-femme" scenario of gay relationships is rare, if not altogether extinct, these days. Male couples do not operate on the *La Cage aux Folles* principle, comforting as that might be to heterosexuals struggling to make sense of homosexual couplings. It has been shown repeatedly that we are far more likely to base our relationship on the "best friend" model, a far superior arrangement that produces an egalitarian framework in which to function. It might not completely eradicate power struggles within a relationship, but it certainly reduces them significantly. Imagine it: you and your partner are best friends, with the added bonus of romantic love and sex. Surely this has advantages over the traditional heterosexual model, which frequently reduces the woman to the status of a subordinate - she may become dependent on her partner financially which leads her to tolerate all kinds of abuses, physical and emotional. How many women wish they could be best friends with their husband instead of being his drudge and servant - and occasionally his punch bag?

## Normal? Natural? What Does It All Mean?

The criticism that gay couples don't produce children is often put forward as proof that same-sex couples are unnatural. This completely ignores the fact that heterosexual couples are often childless - either by choice or by misfortune. Who would have the effrontery to say that their marriages are meaningless because they are infertile? And by whose standards are gay relationships unnatural? I take 'unnatural' to mean something which does not occur in nature. Homosexual partnerings have been recorded throughout history—mostly disapprovingly—but now that we have the courage and the confidence to make these relationships more profound and meaningful to us, we are accused of defying nature. Homosexuality has been recorded as occurring in many animal species, too, which is more than can be said of the Christian religion which has lead the way in persecuting gay people. How many dolphins have you seen reading the Bible or burning their fellows at the stake? Yet affectionate homosexual bonding has been frequently recorded between these intelligent mammals.

As the world becomes increasingly overcrowded it will soon be seen as a virtue not to add further human beings to the total already here. Then, the idea that partnerships are solely for reproduction will seem even more unconvincing.

## Will Coupledom Make Me Any Happier?

The bottom line for most people thinking about entering a partnership is whether it will improve the quality of their life. Will they be any happier than they are as a single person? There has been some objective research into this matter (William and Weinberg "Male homosexuals: their problems and adaptations" - New York / Oxford 1974) which compared gay couples with gay singles and found that, on the whole, the couples were less worried about public intolerance of their sexual behaviour, had more self-esteem and were less guilty and depressed.

## The Persistent Urge

If homosexuality had not been so cruelly persecuted down the centuries would gay partnerings have been common long before now? Some brave souls have tried in the past, and many have sustained their homosexual friendship even in the face of persecution. Take this example, extracted from the memoirs of Rudolf Hoess, commandant of Auschwitz, the Nazi concentration camp:

> "Homosexuals were employed in the clay pit of the large brickworks...Neither the hardest work nor the strictest supervision was of any use in these cases. Whenever they found the opportunity they would fall into each other's arms...Should one lose a 'friend' through sickness or death then the end could be at once foreseen. Many would commit suicide. To such natures, in such circumstances,

11

the 'friend' meant everything. There are instances
of 'friends' committing suicide together."

Even in the grip of such cruel torment, these gay men still
tried to love each other, and it has been the same wherever
repression has been imposed. In the original *Gay News* the
personal contact advertising was prefaced with the quotation
"Love knoweth no locksmiths" as a rebuke to those who
would try to keep gay people from each other. Gay love
cannot be legislated out of existence, it cannot be beaten or
persecuted out of existence. Individual gay people can be
punished, imprisoned or killed, but there will always be
others who will take their place. In Cuba the dictator Fidel
Castro once attempted to deport all the gay men from the
island. Such a project was futile - for even if he had
managed to identify all gay men and put them on board a
ship, his heterosexual population would, even as the ship set
sail, be busily producing another generation of gays.
Homosexuality still exists in Cuba - gay men still find each
other, still make love and still defy the dictator, despite the
possible consequences. They will still be on the island when
Castro is a footnote in history.

Examine, too, the relationship between Violet Trefusis
and Vita Sackville-West, which scandalised literary circles
in the early twenties. The two women had known each other
since they were children, and had become lovers in later
life. However, the conventions of the day could not endure
this, and the two were forcibly returned to their husbands.
But their passion for each other endured. In a letter to Vita,
Violet Trefusis wrote: "I've given my body time after time
to treat as your pleasure, to tear into pieces if such had been
your will...You are my lover and I am your mistress and
kingdoms and empires and governments have tottered and

12

succumbed before now to that mighty combination." However harsh their circumstances, gay people will always find each other, even if they have to hide their love from a hostile society.

There are some experiences in life which are too important to be denied, and intimacy with another human being is one such imperative. For the majority it is accepted that such loving impulses are desirable and to be encouraged, but some people would selfishly try to deny such experiences to the gay minority. The disapproval of the ignorant, though, is not a reason to be excluded from the rich experience of love and companionship that a long-term gay relationship can bring. More and more gay men are trying it and finding they like it. Their loyalty to their partner overtakes their desire to conform. Like lovers down the ages, gay men must love, and there is no insurmountable reason why they shouldn't. In the Western world in the late twentieth century there is more understanding of gay people - our existence is at least acknowledged, even if it is not universally approved. Gay male and lesbian couples up and down the country are living happily and openly. Never before has there been such opportunity to be free from the myth that gay men cannot make full and profound loving relationships together. In their book "Homosexuality in Perspective" (Little, Brown 1979), sexologists Masters and Johnson have concluded that in some respects gay couples have advantages over their straight counterparts. They have maintained that the "social opprobrium" that society heaps upon gay couples can actually strengthen our unions.

We can build on these advantages.

This book is dedicated to those gay men who want to make their relationship work. It is for those who want to share their love and their life with another human being, albeit one of the same sex.

It isn't easy, but if you accept that there will be bad times as well as good and that life will be frustrating as well as fulfilling, then little stands in the way of your finding happiness with the man you love.

# Chapter One:
# Glad to be gay?

**"I Am The Person My Mother Warned Me About"**

So read the lapel badge that was popular in the early seventies when the modern Gay Liberation Movement was in its infancy. That simple phrase startlingly illustrates one of the main reasons why many homosexual men have such a poor self-image and low self-esteem. If even our own mothers are prepared to tell us that gay is evil - however well-intended it may have been - what hope have we of becoming well-adjusted human beings in later life? And how will we ever be able to love another person of the same sex if we believe that not only are *we* evil but our love is corrupt?

## Making Gay Relationships Work

Even if we haven't accepted the idea that we are wicked, there are many other negative images that people are happy to foist upon us. At an early age such ideas can easily lodge in our subconscious, ready to torment us for years to come. Another popular stereotype is that gays are pathetic creatures who are more to be pitied than blamed ("why do they call themselves 'gays' when they are anything but?"). If that doesn't appeal then what about the one that says gay men are hilarious, put on earth simply to entertain and amuse heterosexuals?

For straight people these images are easy to accept because they don't have any direct consequence upon their own lives. For homosexuals, though, they can be fearsomely destructive. Their insidious effects are all around: every time we open a newspaper we are likely to read another stereotyped perception of gay men. Take this, written by John Junor, a British journalist of notorious reactionary opinions: "My own intense dislike of the grotesquely named 'gay' movement is not directed at homosexuals who suffer their infirmity in silence but at those who sleazily flaunt it almost as a badge of honour and seek to pervert the innocent young." In that single sentence you have every popular myth about homosexuality brazenly expressed: the gay man as sick; the gay man as sleazy; the gay man as flaunter; the gay man as child molester.

We have been subjected to this relentless hatred all our lives, whether in the school playground, our youth club, church or home. We would be lucky indeed if at an impressionable age, when it really mattered, we had someone who was prepared to reassure us that it was OK to be gay. Is there really any wonder that so many gay men carry a heavy burden of self-hate?

It's often said that you cannot love another person until you love yourself, and indeed it is a self-evident truth. Those who have tried over and over again to make their relationships with other men work, but always seem to fail, might well become disillusioned. But often their analysis of the failure reaches the wrong conclusion. Instead of asking, as they usually do: "Why don't gay relationships ever last?" They might more usefully ask how they truly feel about their sexuality. Could it be that they *still* consider themselves to be the person their mother warned them about?

Research carried out at the South Bank Polytechnic in London (Project Sigma, 1990) revealed that of 930 gay men who were questioned only 1.8 per cent "regretted a great deal" that they were gay; 67.1 per cent didn't regret it at all; 20.7 per cent regretted it "very little" and 10.7 per cent "regretted it somewhat". But these apparently optimistic figures don't tell us how effectively the subjects of this research deal with their doubts, or where the regret originates. Nor does it tell us what consequences even a small amount of regret can have upon otherwise balanced individuals.

It is fairly obvious that if you still harbour that nagging feeling of discomfort with your sexuality, then there is work to be done. Until you increase your self-esteem as a gay man, you will have much more difficulty forming satisfactory gay relationships.

## Hidden Oppressions

Recently I counselled a young gay man who wanted desperately to have a lover with whom he could make a relationship and live quietly and, he hoped, happily ever after. He was an attractive person, presentable with a pleasing personality. He admitted that he had little trouble finding potential partners, and often allowed himself to be picked up in gay clubs, but seldom initiated the encounters himself. However, even when he met a man with whom he felt he could make a greater commitment, he always spoiled the affair by becoming argumentative or sulky and distant, driving his lovers away with his maddening behaviour. He told me he had allowed several promising opportunities slip through his fingers. It was only after I had seen him for a few sessions that he began to explore the reasons for his inability to sustain long-term relationships. "I realised after a while I always began to feel a bit contemptuous of the men I met. It was a strange thing really, but however pleasant they were and however much I liked them, I kept thinking they were inferior, not like real men. If they liked me, and wanted to make love to me, then they couldn't possibly be any good."

It was some time later that he gained the insight that changed the way he thought about himself. One day he suddenly said: "I don't like the idea of being gay, and I don't think gay relationships are real, because gay people can't live together like a man and a woman can."

When asked where he had got these ideas and why he believed them, he was unable to say. He simply insisted that that was how he felt. He then began to talk about his attitude to his sexuality, how he had been a very unhappy child and adolescent because he had excluded himself from his peer group; he felt his homosexuality made him different. He had been lonely and isolated and only in the last three years had he come to accept that he was gay and ought to do something about it. He had imagined, he said, that when he found Mr Right he would feel happier about his sexual orientation and things would improve. After all, the fantasy of having a strong and thoughtful lover who would take care of him had been with him for most of his life. The problem was that he had not properly explored his attitudes to himself. In his own mind he was still very much the person his mother had warned him about. His experiences on the gay scene with a variety of other people had not been able to shift the anti-gay mythology that had lodged in his mind as a child. Indeed, some of his encounters had actually reinforced it. Sometimes he had tried to make relationships with other men who felt even worse about themselves than he did. These negative influences had done nothing to reassure him that what he felt was unreasonable or self-oppressive.

I asked him about his attitudes to gay life, and there seemed to be much that he despised about his fellow homosexuals. He did not like politically active gays, he did not like "screaming queens", he thought those men he met on the commercial scene were "shallow" and those in the closet "weak". As he articulated all these opinions he was visibly shocked that so much hatred and contempt was emerging from him, for he had many gay friends who fell into the categories he was denigrating.

I waited until he had finished and then, quite spontaneously, he said: "I think the reason I don't like all these people is because they remind me too much of myself."

## To Move or Stay Still?

There is little doubt that the way gay men perceive their sexuality follows an identifiable pattern. It might happen at different times to each of us, but it happens in a very similar way. Some people say they always knew they were gay and can't remember a time when it wasn't part of their consciousness. Others say that they only discovered the fact later in life - sometimes quite a lot later - and found it difficult to accommodate the knowledge into a lifestyle that had become settled and fixed.

One researcher, an Australian psychologist called Vivienne Cass, proposed a model of how gay identity forms, which was published in The Journal of Homosexuality (Spring, 1979). She listed six stages which take the gay individual from not realising he is sexually different from his peers right through to being a well-adjusted homosexual, who has assimilated his sexuality into his whole lifestyle. In between there are several stages of denial and adjustment, some more extreme than others.

Here is a summary of the six stages:

## Stage 1. *Identity Confusion*

From never having considered it, the Stage 1 individual suddenly begins to privately feel that information about homosexuality is somehow personally relevant to him. Try as he may to deny it - and quite often he will try mightily - the confusion and doubts persist. People at this stage sometimes cope with their fear-inducing feelings by becoming anti-gay 'moral crusaders'. They feel that if they condemn homosexuals long enough and loud enough, no-one will suspect that they are themselves gay. Those people at this self-denying point in their development have several other coping strategies. The favourite is by having gay sex, but not getting involved in the experience. They can then make excuses which rationalise their actions: "I was drunk." or "It was just an experiment."

Eventually most people at this stage begin to let down their resistance to the truth and begin to seek further information which will allow them to move on to...

## Stage 2. *Identity Comparison*

Here the individual has consciously accepted that he is homosexual, but devalues the knowledge in order not to lose prestige with important heterosexuals in his life ("I might occasionally have gay feelings but that doesn't make me a homosexual"). At this stage many gay men enter into heterosexual marriage in order to conceal or deny their sexuality. They may, at the same time, be conducting a secret gay sex life. They will try very hard to avoid anything which might 'give the game away' and they may become super-macho. However, if any of these concealment strategies breaks down (for instance, if his wife should discover the truth or he can no longer sustain the tissue of lies) or if the gay feelings become irresistable, then the person moves on to...

## Stage 3. *Identity Tolerance*

Now the individual will have accepted the truth of his sexuality and be prepared to do something about it. He is very likely to seek out other self-defined gay people and find his way into the gay community. He may begin to feel alienated from important heterosexuals in his life. However, if he receives the right kind of support and positive input, his confidence in his sexuality will begin to grow. The important people in his life are now more likely to be homosexual than heterosexual. As long as he has reasonable social skills and meets positive gay people who will

21

reinforce his growing sense of self-esteem, he will begin to explore further and go on to...

## Stage 4. *Identity Acceptance*

At this stage it is likely that the confusion which has plagued the individual so far ("Who am I? What am I?") will be resolved. He will have accepted that he is homosexual and will be exploring it to the full. However, if he has had mainly bad experiences with the gay community he might still only be partially accepting his homosexuality - considering it to be OK in private, but not to be shared with important heterosexuals in his life. If his experience has been mainly positive he is likely to come out to family and friends and to find homophobic attitudes actively offensive. In order to deal with his anger at this perceived injustice, he moves on to...

## Stage 5. *Identity Pride*

Here a person becomes more and more involved in the gay community and the heterosexuals in his life will become less important. It is at this stage that the anger felt by the individual at the injustices meted out by society to homosexuals can cause him to take up gay politics and campaigning. He becomes disillusioned with straights and withdraws further into gay life. He begins to divide the world into gays (who are OK) and straights (who aren't). He will probably feel less and less inclined to hide his sexuality.

However, should his beliefs about the general hostility of heterosexuals be confounded (for instance, if he finds those he comes out to are supportive and accepting), he will move on to....

## Stage 6. *Identity Synthesis*

Finally the idea that "they" (heterosexuals) are the persecutors and "we" (gays) the persecuted, is modified or completely abandoned. Positive experiences with supportive heterosexuals will have broken down the hostility and the individual's gayness can be totally integrated into his wider life. His sexuality is no longer an issue of internal conflict.

I'm sure that most of us will see ourselves somewhere along the continuum described by Vivienne Cass. Naturally in paraphrasing Ms Cass's findings I have had to leave out some of the variations which she included. Gay lives come out of many influences, and Vivienne Cass's model is not meant to represent a blueprint - it is simply a broad idea of how most gay people progress.

The further along the continuum we are, the better the prospect of the relationship succeeding.

We said in the previous chapter that men in gay partnerships tended to have a better self-image and be more confident in their sexuality than those who were not. The greater your degree of self-acceptance the better your partnership's chance of surviving. Being in a good relationship might help your confidence grow, but you would have needed to value your sexuality quite highly in order to get the whole thing off the ground in the first place.

Dominic found himself in such a situation. He had spent many years coming to terms with his homosexuality, having been trained for the priesthood he had come to the painful conclusion that such a life was not for him. He found his way on to the gay scene and rapidly grew in confidence and became happier with his sexuality. Eventually he met Cliff, a man whose gentleness attracted him. They tried to make a relationship together, but Cliff was still at a very early stage in his explorations and was insecure about his orientation. Dominic tells what happened:

"We went about on the gay scene and had a good time and grew closer all the time. Cliff would always come back to my flat for the night and we made love a lot. But he never invited me back to his place. When I asked why this was, he was evasive. I began to wonder what he was hiding, because I knew he lived alone, so there was no problem with other people at the flat. Eventually I confronted him about it, and after a lot of pressure, he admitted that he didn't invite me to his home in case the neighbours saw me going in and asked questions about who I was and why I was staying overnight.

This attitude was devaluing our relationship and I also began to notice that Cliff was making disparaging remarks about some of our gay friends. He wasn't 'out' to many people and seemed almost paranoid about his family finding out.

I told him that unless he began to respect our relationship, and stop making nasty comments about other people's gayness, we would have to go our separate ways. He didn't seem to understand what I was talking about, so we split up. We were apart for about six months, then we met again and he asked if we could have another go. He told me that he had thought hard about what I had said, and now felt that I was right. He's much more open about us now and I think he's making progress."

Dominic and Cliff were a classic example of two people at different stages of development. Although it was a painful time, Dominic's refusal to compromise may well have helped Cliff move along a stage.

## How We Disown Ourselves

In his book "The Disowned Self" (Nash Publishing, 1972), Dr Nathaniel Brandon says: "When a person represses certain aspects of his personality which seem incompatible with the standards of his 'significant others', because he has tied his sense of personal worth to the approval of those 'others', he disowns part of himself." And the cost of disowning essential parts of your personality are a low self-esteem and even active self-hatred. You might seem the best-adjusted person in the world to everyone who knows you, but only you can truly say whether that sense of incompleteness has been mastered or whether it still troubles you and makes you feel unhappy.

Until you are happy to be homosexual, you can't be part of a happy gay couple. If you don't like your sexuality, then there is little possibility that you will be able to successfully share it with another man.

The oft-repeated cry from homosexual men who have failed to make their relationships work is "Gay men are so fickle, they just aren't cut out for long-term relationships." But is this just an excuse because you (or your partner) cling to the idea that you are really, underneath all the charm, *still* the person your mother warned you about? If gay is bad, how can a gay relationship be good?

Your gayness is unlikely to be the reason why your relationships haven't worked out. More likely is that you've simply chosen the wrong man, or that you are clinging to negative ideas of your sexual identity. So this chapter is aimed at helping you look at your attitudes to your homosexuality, to gay lifestyles and to your own self-image. Let's start by examining some of the ways in which gay people oppress themselves.

Gay men who are denying the essential truth of their sexuality become masters of deception - deceiving not only others, but often themselves. An expressionless face covers a multitude of conflicting emotions. We learn at an early age to mask our anger, our hurt and our passion. We become experts at non-reaction, and in the process we stifle and suffocate much of our spontaneity. We don't give much away about ourselves - each piece of information is put through the self-censoring process to ensure that no clue about our secret self is revealed.

## Becoming Whole

The consequences of separating ourselves from such an important part of our personality might manifest itself in such symptoms as mental illness, social inadequacy, deep unhappiness or depression. The constant battles and inner conflicts can, for some individuals, result in emotional devastation, even in these supposedly more enlightened times.

So, how do we go about reclaiming this disowned self so that we can become whole, so that we can live our lives fully? How can we stop this alienation interfering with our desire to love and be loved? Some people will be reading this book because they are not satisfied with the way their sexuality fits in with the rest of their lives. Changing this takes courage, determination and an unflagging commitment to your own growth. It means taking responsibility for yourself and your decisions. It means having confidence in the decisions and actions that you take. It means asserting your right to love in the way that is appropriate for you and which will make you happiest - even if others don't agree.

If you are to bcome a whole human being, you are going to have to say (and mean): "I am master of my own destiny. I make my own decisions and I accept responsibility for them. I will forgive myself if I make mistakes, but I will never again allow others to dictate the course of my life."

## The Sex Machine

Someone who has become separated from essential parts of his personality may become little more than a work machine or a sex machine. The fear of expressing homosexuality in an intimate, emotional way can lead some of us to seek solace in sex as the only real means of reaching out to other people; casual sex becomes a substitute for genuine intimacy. But sex on this level, although superficially exciting, can actually intensify those vague but debilitating sensations of loneliness, particularly in gay men who will not come to terms with their sexuality.

The persistent charge that many homosexual men are "promiscuous", although often loaded and judgmental, is not entirely without foundation. I do not wish to criticise anyone's healthy exploration of their erotic life, but there is little doubt that some gay men use sex as a barrier and an escape.

## *Making Gay Relationships Work*

We must be careful not to fall into the trap of seeming pious or condemnatory; the sexual impulse is strong and I do not wish to suggest that its expression "just for fun" is wrong. My point is that when casual or anonymous encounters, with no balancing involvement, are *all* that a person is capable of having, then that person has surely disowned an important part of himself. Often men in this situation feel a deep sense of loneliness. Despite the brief high that can be experienced after a successful sexual encounter, there is also usually a nagging feeling deep down that life must surely have more meaning. As Ashley Montagu says in his book *Touching:* "It is highly probable that the frenetic pre-occupation with sex that characterizes Western culture is in many cases not the expression of a sexual interest at all, rather a search for the satisfaction of the need for contact."

David is 32. He moved to London ten years ago from Scotland. He told his family he was moving because of the greater work opportunities, but the real reason was so that he could express his homosexuality more easily.

"It was wonderful at first. I was a reasonably attractive youth and had no problems finding sex. I was like the proverbial 'kid let loose in the candy store' and had a long string of brief encounters. I thought in my naïve little way that this was what gay life was about - fucking with everybody I fancied and then moving on. Like everyone else, I kept saying I was looking for the right man to love, but of all the hundreds of men I slept with, none of them seemed like the one. Or if they did seem right I'd find an excuse not to see them again. I broke a few hearts in those days by having affairs and as

28

soon as people starting getting close, I'd run off
and start sleeping around again. Looking back, I
was a bit of a bastard really. It gave me a sort of
power-kick to be able to get people panting and
then walk away from them. It's only recently that I
began to get worried about what I was doing:
spending every night in bars and clubs, always on
the lookout for someone to pick up and take home.
I realise that I'm lucky not to have been infected
with HIV considering the kind of life I've lead.
Although I've got lots of friends on the gay scene I
don't feel close to any of them. If I have sex with
someone, I don't seem to be able to make a
friendship as well. I don't want to see them again
when I've slept with them. Also the people I count
as friends are either straights or gay people who I
don't find physically attractive.

When I got to thirty it began to dawn on me
that I was lonely. It was a strange, niggling feeling
that I couldn't quite pin down. A little voice inside
me was saying 'There's got to be something better
than this', but I couldn't work out what it was. I
started getting depressed and losing interest in just
about everything. In the end I went to see a
psychologist for counselling. He told me I was
afraid of intimacy. I thought he was mad
considering the number of men I'd shared my body
with over the years, but after I'd thought about it, I
began to see what he meant. He wasn't referring to
the physical intimacy, but the more loving type of
closeness. I thought about the number of times I'd
woken up in the morning after picking someone up,
seeing him there in bed beside me and thinking:

'How can I get him out of the flat in the shortest possible time?' I didn't feel anything for any of them. I was kidding myself that these encounters constituted a love life. There wasn't any love - only sex. Most of the time I wouldn't even let them kiss me.

The psychologist told me that there were an awful lot of unresolved issues in my life and if I faced up to them and analysed them it might make me feel better about myself. He told me that I wasn't really happy being homosexual. Despite the fact that I was heavily into gay activism and fund-raising for Aids, I didn't accept that I was valuable on a deeper level. It's true that I've never told my family about being gay, and I'm not 'out' at work with my colleagues. In fact I'm in the closet most of the day. My counsellor also got me to admit that I treat my gay friends differently to my straight ones. I make insulting remarks about them, which are supposed to be jokey, but sometimes I suppose my feelings border on contempt. It sounds very nasty, and I don't express it directly, it just sort of comes out in a disrespectful attitude, as though I don't value them as much as I value straight people. When the psychologist told me this I thought back to something Quentin Crisp had written in his book 'The Naked Civil Servant'. He said he thought any heterosexual, however low and vicious, was superior to any homosexual, however noble. I had thought at the time that this was a terrible thing to say but really, underneath it all, it was something I believed myself. The shrink said I might be able to fool the outside world into

30

thinking I was glad to be gay but I couldn't fool
myself. I think he's got a point."

David made a lot of progress but even though he recognises
the problem, he still has a lot of difficult decisions to make.
The painful and persistent sensation of isolation, which has
been his constant companion over the past ten years, is now
out in the open and there is the opportunity to neutralise it
and move on.

David had been suffering a severe case of low self-
esteem. Only through the constant reassurance of the power
he has to attract other men for sex had he been able to
maintain the falsehood that he is at one with himself. Self-
esteem cannot be nourished by deceit, denial or self-abuse.

Another reason some men seek anonymous sex with
strangers is because they are afraid of the consequences of
real intimacy. Dr. Bernard Zilbergeld expressed it this way
in his book *Men and Sex*:

"In growing up, girls more than boys were allowed
to express and explore their desire for physical
contact. Having the permission, girls learned to
differentiate their needs for support, comfort,
validation and a sense of connection with another,
and similar needs from the need for sex. Boys
developed in the opposite direction. Wanting sex
was legitimate, even encouraged, while such things
as wanting to be held or loved or to know they
were not alone were unacceptable...Wanting to hug
or to feel close to another sounded too effeminate,
but wanting sex was the epitome of masculinity;
and in sex you could get some of these other things
as well. After years of practice, the man just never

felt the need for closeness or comfort or support. All he needed was - sex. Whenever he wanted something that might be called warm or close or loving, he read it as a desire for - sex."

## The Work Machine

Christopher, on the other hand, found that work provided a substitute for the uncomfortable truths he was avoiding. Through constant striving and endless hours of effort he rose, in a very short time, to dizzy heights in the business world. His career was looked on with admiration and amazement by colleagues who just couldn't keep up. Christopher would get up at six, go to the office at seven, stay there until well after ten in the evening and then, after a quick drink at the local pub, would return to his flat and prepare for the following day's effort.

"In many ways I had nothing else in my life but work. I took on more and more responsibility, my working hours became longer - ensuring that at weekends I worked almost constantly at home. I never allowed myself to become sick - somehow I overcame colds and ignored minor illnesses as though they weren't happening. Nothing could stop me going into the office. I was totally involved and life was a constant round of telephone calls, meetings, negotiations, hirings and firings. I never delegated. Even the small amount of social life that I had was connected with work, whether entertaining clients or going to dinner parties at the homes of colleagues and their wives. These events were hardly ever pleasurable, more like duty.

People kept telling me that I was overdoing it, and I knew they were right. But I couldn't stop. In a way I daren't stop. If I spent time ill in bed I suppose I would have started thinking about what I was doing with my life, and that wasn't something I could allow to happen. So I just kept going. But occasionally, when I was forced to pause momentarily - stuck in a traffic jam or on a long plane journey - the thought would cross my mind that I didn't have any real friends, and nothing happened to me at all in my personal life, except the occasional phone call to my mother.

I told myself I was reluctant to make any commitments outside of work in case they interfered with my schedule but, of course, the real reason was that I didn't know what I wanted. I knew I was gay, for instance, but I was afraid to do anything about it - it would complicate matters at work if I had a 'private life'. The commercial world is a very conservative one and isn't very tolerant of people who aren't conventional. In business they like you to be married and settled. I think at 35 they still considered me young enough to 'do the right thing', but my commitment to the firm was such that no-one ever thought to question any other aspect of my life; I had made myself invaluable to them, they always got 150 per cent effort.

But then these feelings of missing out on life became more and more insistent. I was chatting in the staff canteen with one of my colleagues who was always telling me that I was a fool, working myself into the ground and stuff like that. His favourite saying was 'The graveyards are full of indispensable people.' He said: 'You know you're an eligible bachelor, don't you? Pots of money stashed away, nice house, not bad looking. There are a few women in the firm who wouldn't mind getting their feet under your table. Why don't you think about it?'

The prospect terrified me. I knew enough about myself to realise that I couldn't make a successful relationship with a woman. I occasionally found myself fancying some of the men I saw around the place—and I occasionally used them in my wank fantasies—but I never did anything about it. Too dangerous. The more I thought about it - and I thought about it increasingly once the process got started - the more I realised that I was avoiding the issue. This obsession with work was as much to do with avoiding my sexuality as with ambition to succeed. And yet I had no idea what else to do.

It all came to a head when I realised that one of the younger men in the accounts department was being more than usually friendly. Generally I wouldn't have noticed, but I had begun to tune myself into his signals, if you know what I mean. I had opened myself up a little, taken my nose out of the company books for five minutes to take a furtive peep at the world. Even so, I was reluctant to pursue this man's rather obvious attentions; the possible complications didn't seem worth it. All the same, I was becoming incredibly depressed. I'd never felt like that before. I decided that the next time this young man started dropping hints I would follow it up.

It didn't take long and I took the plunge. We went out for a drink together and then back to his flat. I was most embarrassed to tell him that I was a virgin with both women and men. However, we had sex and it was very pleasant, although obviously not the romance of the century. We became friends, though, and he taught me a lot about myself. He made me realise how important life outside of work can be - not just for the social aspects, but for the sense of completeness a love life can provide. I loosened up a bit and went out on the gay scene with him. I became less intense about my career and less afraid of my feelings. I was more interested in what else life had to offer. Eventually I started a more serious relationship with Daniel, who has moved into my house. We live a quiet life, but I can assure you that he has given me a whole new insight into what being alive is about. This is what I have been avoiding all these years, the very thing that makes me happiest. Crazy isn't it?"

## Increasing Gay Self-Esteem

If you are refuting essential aspects of yourself - and your sexuality is indeed essential to your emotional welfare - then you cannot feel good about yourself. In the back of your mind there is always the undermining thought that you are unworthy, valueless or even evil. There is a constant anxiety about what people will think about you if they should ever discover who you *really* are. Only by confronting the fears that create this alienation can you become whole.

## *Making Gay Relationships Work*

Later in this chapter we will look at some of the excuses and rationalisations which gay people use to reinforce their determination not to face up to the fact that they are hurting themselves psychologically. These are the surface defence mechanisms which they have invented to maintain the fiction that we are not really essentially different from our "significant others". Our defensive rationalisations may deflect other people's disapproval, but they cannot protect us from the dreadful hollow feeling of "not belonging" that can be created by our estrangement from ourselves. You cannot rationalise the constantly denied need for intimacy - it cries out from a more primitive depth.

### How We Rationalise Our Self Oppression

Most gay people who have grown up in a state of fear and been exposed to unalleviated negative indoctrination will become socially or emotionally maladjusted to some extent. It may not be immediately apparent that our fears and uncertainties about our sexuality are affecting the way we function in the world. Indeed, many gay people are wildly successful in their chosen sphere of life - in art, business, the caring professions, teaching or whatever, but they are deeply unhappy and confused about their private lives.

The conflicts which arise in connection with sex, intimacy and loving relationships can be shattering. Those who have internalised these profound doubts about their sexual orientation may well be able to pursue their career with a vengeance; but without a satisfying emotional life, balance may be absent. This distrust of one's deepest feelings can manifest itself in many ways: a constant search for anonymous sex, perhaps, or an inability to make emotional commitments. Passing for straight can lead to unhappy homosexuals getting married in order to cover up the truth or as a genuine attempt to escape from it. Disillusion and bitterness are often the result, probably for both parties.

At this point, the reader might throw up his hands and say: this does not apply to me. I am well-adjusted, socially acceptable and at peace with myself. But do you include your homosexuality in that statement? Can you hold up your head and say that even if you aren't exactly glad to be gay you are at least not hostile to it? As the German film director Rosa von Praunheim put it: "Gay people are used to using every available corner to hide in. We've spent so many years of our lives learning to hide. In the face of Aids we need to be more open about our sexuality than ever before. If we live in a democracy then individuals should have the power to change things, and to take part in the changes that take place. We have to be more aware, to show personal courage. It is not enough to escape into glossy magazines or discos."

## Justifying The Status Quo

Look at the following list of six statements. Would you say that you subscribe to them, or variations of them:

1. "I don't need to tell people I'm gay. My sex life is nobody's business but my own."

2. "I think the gay liberation movement does more harm than good. It just upsets heterosexuals and turns them against us."

37

3 "Just because I'm attracted to members of my own sex doesn't mean I want to be labelled as gay, bisexual or anything else. I'm just a human being."

4. "I wouldn't go on gay demonstrations. I don't think it's necessary to shout it from the rooftops."

5. "I hate these effeminate gay men who wear make-up and dresses and parade around flaunting their sexuality."

6. "Children at school shouldn't be taught about homosexuality - if they are exposed to it at an early age it might influence the way they develop."

All these statements might appear, on the surface, perfectly reasonable and moderate; they seem to reflect a desire not to make our sexuality into a 'cause'. But if we examine them more closely we will see they are shot through with misunderstandings, half-truths and self-delusions. Let's re-run them and look at them from another point of view:

*1. "I don't need to tell anyone I'm gay. My sex life is no-one else's business."*

Another variation on this theme is: 'Heterosexuals don't stuff their sex lives down my throat, why should I do it to them?' But heterosexuals *do* force their sex lives on to us, just about every minute of the day. We see men and women in sexual situations on television and in feature films, we read about their sexual activities in newspapers and books. When men and women get married or live together, the implication is that it is for sexual as well as other reasons ("With my body I thee worship"). Anyone who wears a wedding ring is announcing to the world that he or she has sex with their spouse. It's unlikely that these people would want to tell you in detail what they do in bed - what positions they favour, how much time they spend in foreplay, whether they like oral sex and so on. Telling someone you are married does not mean that you will talk about your bedroom activities, but it does imply that there *is* a sexual relationship between you and your partner. By the same token, saying that you are living in a gay relationship is not the same as describing the details of your sexual activities. It just acknowledges that there are some.

2. *"I think the gay liberation movement does more harm than good. It just upsets heterosexuals and turns them against us."*

What this really means is: "However unjust and ignorant heterosexuals are, however abysmally they behave towards gay people, we must not protest lest we upset them further." It seems to say that we must tolerate heterosexuals sacking us from our jobs, sending us to prison because we love someone of the same sex, vilifying us in newspapers, assaulting us on the streets, evicting us from our homes and so on. By this same reasoning no-one must ever speak out against these flagrant abuses of human rights, in case the gay-bashers become even more upset.

This casts us in the role of victim - not a good base for confidence-building. We must, if we accept the statement, tolerate whatever unfair action is taken by the majority. The opinions of those who wish to persecute homosexuals are often based on sheer prejudice and ignorance. There is no good reason to give credence to such opinions. After all, if someone told lies about some other aspect of your life—say that you were a thief or a persistent liar—the likelihood is that you would want to contradict them. The fact that they are talking about homosexuality—a concept which we often deny has anything to do with us—means that we are prepared to tolerate their ignorance, even though it affects us adversely. But remember, if a threat is posed to homosexuals in general, it will eventually find its way to you in particular. Why should we not protest when there is a direct threat to our happiness and safety?

If you haven't had direct experience of anti-gay discrimination it is easy to form the impression that those who have are exaggerating. We can find excuses for not sympathising ("They shouldn't flaunt it / be so strident / make so many demands etc.") but if someone has been abused solely because of their homosexuality, then it is an abuse of all gay people. Only the time, the place and the circumstances made it happen to them and not to you.

Keeping quiet about discrimination simply invites a repeat. The introduction of Section 28 in Britain indicated that there is a strong anti-gay element at work in our Parliament. If we sit around without protest then this element will feel it has carte blanche to go forward and extend its restrictive measures. And then it won't be someone else who is getting the sharp end of the stick, it will be all of us. Including you.

*3. "Just because I'm attracted to members of my own sex doesn't mean I want to be labelled homosexual or bisexual or anything else. I'm just a human being."*

You are indubitably a human being first and a homosexual human being second. Your sexuality, whether straight or gay, is not the only thing in your life. But it is a very important aspect and not one which you can safely pretend does not exist. If your sexual impulses draw you to members of your own sex, and you wish to express yourself in that way, then there is little hope of avoiding the label homosexual or bisexual. What you have to decide is whether you apply the label to yourself or let other people do it for you. If you deny you are gay, even though your actions and emotions say otherwise, this could cause severe emotional problems. By embracing the truth about your sexuality, you can open up your emotional life in a way that will satisfy you and allow you to grow. If you deny your gayness in order to avoid the hatred of bigots, you are allowing these very bigots to limit your chances of love and success. Take for instance this, written for the *Sunday Telegraph* by Roger Scruton, a professor of "aesthetics" and a leading right-wing "intellectual":

"A certain number of people in any generation, especially men, are attracted to their own sex, and in particular the young of their own sex. This attraction is not uncommon and traditional morality ensured that it would be useful. Homosexual feelings were overcome - 'sublimated' - and turned to larger uses. Those who experienced them sought an outlet in *paideia* (as the Greeks called it): they became priests, teachers, fathers to everyone's children. Their homosexuality, far from being a threat, became a benefit - a contribution to the social continuity and to the inheritance of future generations. But the benefit depended upon shame and renunciation, which turned lust into charity...The liberated homosexual makes no such

41

sacrifice...The result of this liberation is unprecedented promiscuity."

Mr Scruton infers that because homosexuals can't produce children (which is manifestly untrue) they have no interest in the future and live only for the day. He feels that when homosexuality is accompanied by shame, denial and repression it is useful, but if homosexuals are allowed to be open and free from unhappiness, then trouble ensues. This is an almost unbelievably selfish attitude. He seems to want an appreciable minority of people to live lives of unutterable misery so that *he* does not feel uncomfortable. His assertion that liberated homosexuals contribute nothing to the community is patently ridiculous. Homosexuals are still priests, nurses and teachers - and many of them are parents. What Mr Scruton sees as indulgence is simply an expression of sexuality. And yes, homosexual acts can be exploitative and meaningless - but so can their heterosexual equivalents. After all, the vast majority of rapes are of women by men; most child abuse is perpetrated by heterosexual men on young girls; most prostitutes are women serving heterosexual men. Does Mr Scruton recommend a wholesale condemnation of heterosexuality because of these facts?

Mr Scruton's arguments might be appealing to those people who are looking for some kind of "reasoning" to justify their hatred of homosexuals, but that does not make him right. Homophobia - an irrational aversion to homosexuals - is a condition suffered by many people, including some gay people. Most heterosexuals have no motivation or desire to confront their prejudices and so those prejudices pass unchallenged from one generation to the next. Unless they have personal experience (perhaps because one of their children is gay) straight people can get through life with their homophobia completely unchallenged. They can imagine that the issue of homosexuality has nothing whatsoever to do with them. But homosexuals, and those who are important in their lives, cannot claim that the subject is irrelevant. They cannot afford the complacency so evident in Roger Scruton's complacent writings. Gay people must find the strength to resist these ideas, and we must overcome this fear and loathing of our own kind. If we internalise and believe such grotesquely distorted ideas about our place in the world, we will become the outcasts which Roger Scruton and his ilk believe we ought to be.

*4   "I wouldn't go on a gay demonstration, I don't think it's necessary to shout it from the rooftops."*

Sometimes demonstrations in the streets are the only way to draw attention to injustices. Most revolutions start in such a way, as events in Eastern Europe over the past few years have shown.

The mass media—particularly popular newspapers—do not allow gay people a fair hearing and we have great difficulty bringing our grievances to the attention of the public. If we want to make sure that our voices are heard then parading in the streets is one way of doing it. Many pressure groups use this tactic to get their message across. Why shouldn't gay people use it too?

As for "shouting it from the rooftops", this usually means "I want to stay in the closet because it's safer and less hassle there." Nobody expects any gay man to broadcast the details of his sexuality to the world, but if you want to respect yourself and be free from self-oppression, you need to share the knowledge with your family, friends and others who are close to you. This does not mean "shouting it from the rooftops", it means having respect for yourself as a whole human being. I think there would be something insufferably affected about walking up to a complete stranger and announcing your homosexuality to them. For one thing it has nothing to do with strangers - any more than how much you have in the bank or what kind of breakfast cereal you prefer - but when you like someone, or even love them, then it is appropriate that you should tell them about yourself so that they know what kind of person you are. It is no use trying to have a friendship with someone who assumes you are heterosexual. There is a certain indignity in "going along" with an assumption about yourself which you know is untrue. It robs you, your friends and family of dignity and debases these relationships.

*5. "I hate those effeminate gays who wear make-up and dresses and parade about flaunting their sexuality. "*

Gay men with so-called effeminate mannerisms and speech patterns make a lot of their more conventional brothers feel uncomfortable. Effeminate gay men draw attention to all the things which closeted gay men try to obscure. There is no doubt or ambiguity about effeminate gays. Not only are they saying, by their manner and approach to life, "I am homosexual" they are also saying "and I don't care who knows".

For those who have invested so much energy into hiding this knowledge about themselves, "screaming queens" are a nightmare. Every time such a person lisps or prances, the closet case winces because he knows that under the smoke screen, he too shares the same sexuality and desires as his more obviously gay brother. The gay community consists of an enormous variety of individuals, but there are those among us who try to reject this diversity. Some gay men would prefer to merge themselves into a crowd and convince everyone that they lead the approved and orthodox lifestyle. If they appear to be like everyone else they need not fear becoming an outcast. The desire for conventionality ("passing for straight") indicates a profound unease with their sexuality.

If you find yourself becoming angry when you see effeminate gay men camping it up in a bar or club, ask yourself why. Is it really their behaviour which is annoying you, or is it the uncomfortable truth about yourself which they are forcing you to confront?

*6. "Children at school shouldn't be taught about homosexuality - if they are exposed to it at an early age, it might influence the way they develop."*

This was the argument used by the proponents of the notorious section 28, which the British Government brought into law in 1988. It sought to stop the "intentional promotion of homosexuality in schools."

In order to accept the children-will-be-influenced argument, you first have to accept that there is something intrinsically wrong with being homosexual. If you don't accept that a homosexual lifestyle is automatically wrong, then you can't accept that children shouldn't be told about it. If it is true - and there is no evidence that it is - that these children would experiment with homosexuality, then what is wrong with that? If they want to find out about themselves then it seems like a perfectly good idea. However, they should be reassured that experimenting with

45

homosexual sex doesn't mean they'll turn out to be gay any more than heterosexual experimentation will automatically make them straight. Indeed, ask just about any gay man and he'll tell you that he tried, with varying degrees of success, to have sex with women at some time in his life.

Children should be taught about safer sex, the value of relationships (of whatever kind) and the difficulties created by society's attitudes. That should give them enough information to make up their own minds. They will experiment anyway. According to research by Project Sigma, 87% of the 1,000 gay men they surveyed said they had had their first homosexual experience before they were 20. The average age for the fist sexual experience was 15.7 years. Few, if any, of them had been 'seduced' into homosexuality. The average age difference between partners at the first sexual experience was one year. Most actively sought this first experience, which gives lie to the stupid but persistent idea that older men are 'recruiting' younger men into a gay lifestyle.

Are gay children to be permanently denied information on the options that are open to them in adult life? Are they to be given no reassurance or positive information?

As with any other subject, children should be given the facts without bias or opinion. They will come across gay people at some point in their lives and if they are taught that homosexuals are evil (or, at least, not taught that gay people deserve the same respect as anyone else) they will have totally unnecessary conflicts. Because so many conservative influences hold sway in our education system it is unlikely that children will be allowed to make up their own minds, and the dreadful cycle of homophobia will pass unimpeded from one generation to the next.

We are all exposed to anti-gay brainwashing; we have to listen to it every day. We read that we are "sordid" in the scandal-sheets which pose as newspapers. Our friends might use words like "poofter" or "shirtlifter" without thinking what such words can do to our self-esteem, if we let them.

If we have internalised and accepted these images of our sexuality, then we will be hard pressed to accept our gayness as a positive force for good. You've often heard that homosexuality equals Aids, or that all gay men sexually abuse young boys or that homosexual sex is 'filthy and depraved'. You may have heard such opinions from people you love and respect - your parents, your teacher, your doctor or the vicar. Eventually these messages get through: you are gay and therefore you must be all these other dreadful things, too.

So relentless and pervasive is the process that we don't always realise what is happening. It is unlikely that we've been raised in an atmosphere convivial to homosexual love. It is doubtful that our parents would ever encourage us to "play at being gay" when we are children. In fact, they would probably have spent most of their time discouraging us from any expression which might be considered "homosexual". It is still a strong taboo in our society and it still impels parents to torture their gay children - however unwittingly.

Having absorbed all these doubts and fears about ourselves, many of us deny that we are homosexual. After all, how could we admit to being one of those demons whom everyone seems to hate so intensely? Look at some of the things British newspapers print about us:

"Homosexuals are nothing new...it's just that, when a nation becomes increasingly evil, more of its people and others who are close to you. This does not mean "shouting it from the rooftops", it means having respect for yourself as a whole human being. I think there would be something insufferably affected about walking up to a complete stranger and announcing your homosexuality to them. For one thing it has nothing to do with strangers - any more than how much you have in the bank or what kind of breakfast cereal you prefer - but when you like someone, or even love them, then it is appropriate that you should tell them about yourself so that they know what kind of person you are. It is no use trying to have a friendship with someone who assumes you are heterosexual. There is a certain indignity in "going along" with an assumption about yourself which you know is untrue. It robs you, your friends and family of dignity and debases these relationships.

*5. "I hate those effeminate gays who wear make-up and dresses and parade about flaunting their sexuality."*

Gay men with so-called effeminate mannerisms and speech patterns make a lot of their more conventional brothers feel uncomfortable. Effeminate gay men draw attention to all the things which closeted gay men try to obscure. There is no doubt or ambiguity about effeminate gays. Not only are they saying, by their manner and approach to life, "I am homosexual" they are also saying "and I don't care who knows".

For those who have invested so much energy into hiding this knowledge about themselves, "screaming queens" are a nightmare. Every time such a person lisps or prances, the closet case winces because he knows that under the smoke screen, he too shares the same sexuality and desires as his effects upon the self-esteem of those gay men who are already uncertain and confused. Surrounded by such hostility and without support, you would have to be very strong indeed to recognise and challenge these distorted attitudes.

And yet, even for the most isolated and least aware gay person there will be a little voice deep down inside protesting the injustice of it all. Somewhere, often stifled beyond hearing, the voice is trying to say: "I want to love and be loved. I want my own kind of love."

No love is immoral. Love is simply the most wonderful thing in the world and it transcends the strictures of police, priests, politicians and parents. Nobody has yet found a way to control what goes on inside our heads, nobody has yet managed to shackle our secret desires.

## The Breast-Plate Of Righteousness

Sometimes we ourselves conspire with the authoritarian forces trying to subdue us. Some gay men seem to accept the poisonous opinions of our would-be oppressors and go to great pains not to upset them. Occasionally we can become so convinced by bigoted arguments that we even attack our fellow gays. People who do this have become fixed at Stage One of Vivienne Cass's continuum.

This phenomenon has been identified by the American researcher Laud Humphreys, who called it "The breast-plate of righteousness". The breast-plate is worn by some gay men to conceal their true nature. Such men present themselves to the world as overly respectable and orthodox; the breast-plate wearer becomes intensely illiberal in his opinions and is often highly conservative, both politically and socially. Some of the subjects in Humphreys' study (published as "Tearoom Trade") were even described as "moral crusaders" who encouraged vice squad activity and publicly opposed civil rights for homosexuals.

You don't have to look very far to find examples of such people. Take the case of Roy Cohn, the right-hand man of senator Joe McCarthy, who led the infamous communist witch hunts in the USA during the fifties. Senator McCarthy and his assistant, Cohn, also uncovered many homosexual people working in the American government and hounded them into obscurity, labelling them 'un-American' and 'threats to the nation'. Later, when he died from Aids, it was revealed that Roy Cohn was himself a homosexual man. So deep had been Cohn's hatred of his homosexuality that it had driven him to hurt others as a perverse sort of revenge.

Another prominent example of a homosexual who mercilessly persecuted other homosexuals was J Edgar Hoover, the chief of America's FBI for over forty years. All the time that Hoover was using other people's homosexual orientation to discredit and destroy them, he was leading a life of unconstrained homosexuality himself.

Also in America, the founder of the National Conservative Political Action Committee, Mr Terry Dolan, once mailed a fund-raising letter for his organisation which read: "Our nation's moral fibre is being weakened by the growing homosexual movement." Mr Dolan, too, died from Aids contracted through homosexual activity.

This phenomenon of the breast-plate of righteousness is familiar to gay activists who will often report coming upon other gay men in powerful positions who fiercely resist pro-gay reforms. They become anti-gay for a number of reasons. Cohn and Dolan, unable to accept their own

50

homosexuality, tried to deflect attention from it by destroying others.

There are no reliable figures available, but it is clear that a significant number of gay people (or potentially gay people) are married. Those who have turned against themselves have often made such a good job of it that they don't even know it has happened. But for the gay man who is trying to hide the truth there will be unexpected moments of insight. He may suddenly feel an unsettling spark of desire for a man he sees in the street, or he will be unwillingly excited by the sight of another man's body; without warning a sexual fantasy might conjure up a male-male theme. Terrible doubts might flicker for a second in the mind of such a man, but they will be quickly smothered and be pushed back into the dark depths from whence they came.

We all have to make our own way in the world of love, and we all have to decide who we want to love. Not all of us feel that we can allow ourselves to acknowledge the truth, and not all of us reach the decision at the same point in our lives. Most of us make mistakes on our journey along the continuum.

We have explored here some of the reasons gay people find difficulty in accepting and embracing their sexuality. The depth of the indoctrination we have all received is profound, and it will not be easily overcome. But our task is to turn the hate we may feel for ourselves into love. Raising our self-esteem is the solution.

Once we have reached the stage where we can truly say: "I like myself and I like being gay" then the chances of our being able to successfully enter into a gay relationship are increased a thousandfold.

But how is this to be achieved? How can we move ourselves stage by stage to the point where we are not our own worst enemy? There is no easy route, but you can help yourself by trying to seek out positive gay people who can show you by example that success in gay life is possible. Try to recognise those who are stuck somewhere at the beginning of the continuum, the kind of people who cannot help you to move forward because they haven't yet helped themselves. They are struggling with the same demons that you are. Don't let a few bad experiences sour you to the many good, life-enhancing things that your homosexuality can bring. In other words, don't blame your gayness for your own inability to be perfect.

Read extensively (and can I suggest you begin with my book *Assertively Gay: How to Build Gay Self-Esteem* - The Other Way Press). Expose yourself to positive experiences within the gay community - there are plenty of opportunities. The more you explore, the more you open up, the sooner your self-esteem will increase and the happier you will feel about your lot in life. At that point the prospects for making a successful relationship will have improved immeasurably.

# Chapter Two:

# How do gay couples meet?

It takes two to tango, and before you can make your relationship work, you're faced with the difficult task of actually finding that someone with whom you want to make a life partnership. For some lucky people it happens spontaneously with no planning required. Others long for a regular companion, but just don't seem able to pin down like-minded people.

The frequent cry I hear in counselling sessions with gay men who have not succeeded in finding that special someone is: "Nobody seems to want to settle down, all they want is quick sex." And yet, almost everyone I speak to purports to want (either now or at some time in the future) to find the right man and make a go of it.

So, if you haven't already managed it, how do you find that elusive Mr Right?

Unfortunately there is no formula that will make the task easy; it seems to boil down to equal parts of effort, good judgement and sheer luck. But while much can depend on your being in the right place at the right time, there are some active steps you can take in increasing your chances of finding the partner you are looking for. You can start by creating a frame of mind to ensure that you're giving out the right "vibes" to those around who might be interested. Opening yourself up to possibilities and keeping alert to opportunities increase your chances of achieving the desired result.

The right mind-set should also be accompanied by an effort to put yourself in as many social situations as possible. Mix with as wide a range of people as you can and enjoy them for themselves. (Everyone you meet won't be the man of your dreams, but they are all potential friends.)

There is a danger here of going into overdrive. Because you've decided to actively seek out the man with whom you want to spend your life, you might begin to come over as pushy or - worse still - desperate. Projecting on to unsuitable or unwilling candidates your desire for a commitment can be very embarrassing, and repeated rejections can lead to disillusionment. Most people who have made successful partnerships have found that, although their relationship may have started with a grand passion, the commitment built up gradually over a long period. Few people know at the first meeting that they've just shaken hands (or whatever) with the man they're going to share their life with.

According to research (Project Sigma, 1993), the most frequently-used venues for gay men in search of sexual partners are, in order of popularity: pubs, which were preferred by 35%; clubs (32%); cottages (23%); cruising grounds (18%); saunas (12%); beaches (2%); parties (7%); street (3%). These places were visited with the intention of picking people up for sex rather than seeking a long-term relationship, but who knows where any contact may lead?

To get an idea of where gay people who are already in relationships met, I asked some of the couples who helped with the research for this book how they had got together. Here are some of their stories.

## Andy & Joe

**Andy**: To put it bluntly, Joe and I met through cottaging. I'd only been 'out' to any degree for a few months, and I had no idea where the gay scene was in the town where I was living. But I had discovered when I was younger that you could meet men and have sex in public lavatories. I know it sounds a bit sordid and a lot of people disapprove, but that's all I knew about at the time. Anyway, I thought my luck was in the evening I saw Joe standing there in the loo in the park. He was just the right type for me physically - tall, blond and slender. I made a pass at him and he responded.

**Joe**: I was petrified because it was the first time I had done this sort of thing. I'd been on the gay scene, in the pubs and clubs for a few years, and of course I had heard people talking about the cottages. On this particular day I was feeling in need of a bit of company and I just couldn't be bothered with all the rigmarole in the pub - you know, chatting people up, buying them drinks, worrying that they'll tell you to fuck off because they don't fancy you. I just wanted to get my rocks off. Andy was there, he was interested and so we came back to my place. I suppose I was foolish really to take such a risk, but he looked decent enough. Anyway, we found we got on very well. We had sex, then we had a cup of coffee and a chat. Believe it or not, I enjoyed the coffee and chat best of all.

**Andy:** Then we had sex again. This was the first time I'd ever been back to someone's home from a cottaging troll. I liked it, and Joe was really charming. We enjoyed each other's company so much that I stayed the night.

**Joe:** And after that we saw each other just about every day for the next three weeks, and we got closer and closer. It all blossomed from there, and we've been together since - four years.

**Andy:** It hasn't all been plain sailing, but I wouldn't have missed it for the world, and I hope we've got a lot more years ahead of us. I don't think I'd want to go back to my single life now.

Although Andy and Joe were lucky (and I've spoken to other people who've met through cottages and gone on to make successful relationships), cottaging is an horrendously dangerous activity. Not only do the police regularly stake out notorious cruising places and make literally hundreds of arrests, these rendezvous are also known to local thugs who might want to engage in a bit of gay bashing.

Cottaging has its *aficionados* who say that the risks actually add to the erotic buzz, but most gay men prefer the safer alternatives of pubs, clubs and groups.

## Stan & David

**Stan**: It must be fifteen years since I met David at the local gay pub. In those days it was quite a thrill to see so many gay people together in one place. Nowadays it's nothing to see tens of thousands at the Pride event in London. We were both regulars at this pub, and knew each other by sight. In a small town like this the clientele of the pub doesn't change very much. Anyway, we eventually got together one night and found we sparked each other off.

**David**: It was a strange relationship really. We started by queening it up together - we both like camp humour. We were a couple of screamers egging each other on, and we loved it. We didn't have a sexual relationship at first, we used to call each other sisters. But as we got a bit older, we started to calm down and show a bit of decorum.

**Stan**: I must say I showed a bit more decorum than you did. You're still a bit on the outrageous side.

**David:** Well it was you that had the sex change! I don't mean that literally, he didn't really have a sex change, but he went butch. He stopped camping it up and grew a moustache.

**Stan**: We had so many laughs in those days, we went everywhere together. There isn't a gay club or pub in the British Isles that hasn't been graced by our presence.

**David**: We're both fond of company, and we still go out and about a lot.

**Stan:** Not as much as we used to. We're turning a bit into home birds. Watching Coronation Street and doing flower arrangements.

**David:** We do dinner parties and have our friends around sometimes. I like that - I can go mad with the flowers and the table decorations.

**Stan:** Well you change as you get older, don't you? I can't keep up with the music these days. You go to discos and it all sounds like static on the wireless. I used to know all the music at one time.

**David:** It's the maximum security rest home for us next, I can see it.

Pubs and clubs are excellent meeting places for those who are gregarious, outgoing and have plenty of confidence. A good pair of lungs is also useful as many gay pubs play very loud music, making conversation difficult. The competitive nature of the pub and club scene can make it seem unwelcoming and threatening for those who aren't young, good looking and whose self-esteem isn't strong enough to withstand frequent rejections.

Having said that, most of us spend some time exploring the gay scene, and many of us strike lucky there.

## Gerald & Karl

**Gerald**: It was love over the filing cabinets for us, wasn't it? We met at the office. I was working in the accounts department and he was in the post room.

**Karl**: No I was in the cashiers department by then.

**Gerald**: Anyway, it was a fairly big firm, and I only saw him about every other day. I'd see him in the canteen sometimes, and I'd think to myself how fanciable he was, but I didn't know how I was going to get to know him.

**Karl**: I'd noticed him staring at me. It was dead obvious really. You develop a sort of invisible gay antenna, don't you? I was just picking up these not-so-subtle clues, like the way he stared at me every time we were in the same room, and the way he kept gazing between my legs. I felt as though he was undressing me every time I went to the canteen—you know, the sort of thing women complain about.

**Gerald:** Was it that obvious? I must say you were quite a hunk. And you did put it on display a bit with those worn-out jeans you used to wear.

**Karl:** I'm not complaining. I'm just saying you made it a bit obvious. I decided to let him know I'd noticed, so I started to smile at him. Then one day he was sitting on his own in he canteen, so I asked if I could join him and he said yes.

**Gerald:** I was so nervous I didn't know what to say.

**Karl:** Fortunately I'm not so shy. It didn't take long to suss you out.

**Gerald:** God, when I think about it, you were so brazen.

**Karl:** Only because I knew I was on pretty safe ground. Anyway, within three days we were down there in the archive basement where all the old files were kept and where nobody ever went, having rather nerve-racking sex.

**Gerald:** Then we started to see each other outside work, and after six months we decided to move in together. That is to say, I moved in with Karl. I was living with my parents at the time. We haven't looked back since, have we chuck?

Work is an excellent place to meet potential lovers, especially if you have a job that brings you into contact with lots of people. There are dangers, of course. It's easy for isolated or lonely gay people to develop crushes on attractive straight men who are simply unattainable. There is something about working closely with people that can create a bond of respect and affection that can rapidly turn into sexual attraction. Sometimes it can be expressed, but most of the time it has to be repressed.

Falling in love with a work colleague is very easy. It can be a wonderful thing or a dreadful inconvenience, putting a strain on your working relationship and threatening your career. And, of course, one false move, one misinterpreted signal and you might find yourself at the centre of an unpleasant row which could ultimately result in your losing your job. There have already been several cases of sexual harassment brought before industrial tribunals by straight people who have been propositioned or pestered by gay work colleagues.

The advice is to be realistic in your assessment of potential partners at work, and weigh up the possible consequences before making a move.

## *How do Gay Couples Meet?*

### Personal Ads: Jake and Martin's experience

**Jake**: I've been advertising in the personal columns of newspapers and magazines for years now, and I've met some really nice people this way. The problem is, they were either living miles away or they weren't interested in long-term relationships. I'll admit that I did sometimes advertise just for sexual partners, but somewhere in the back of my mind was this little hope that one of them would turn out to be something more.

Not all the people who replied were pleasant. I got letters from some real weirdoes - I mean, people you'd run a mile from. Sometimes I'd get a stack of replies, and sometimes only one or two. Anyway, the last time I did it, I got a letter from Martin. He only lived a few miles down the road and from what he wrote sounded quite normal. He didn't want to tie me to the bed or piss on me or any of the other things that I find a bit of a turn-off. He also sent a photo of himself which impressed me. He's got a very open face, and I like that. I also like his dark hair and complexion. So I gave him a ring and we arranged to meet in a pub. I wouldn't give anyone my address or invite them to my home until I'd checked them out on neutral ground.

He turned out to be exactly as he'd said in the letter. Quite often the people who wrote weren't anything like I'd imagined from their descriptions of themselves. Either they were deliberately lying or they had a very exaggerated idea of what they looked like. You'd expect the hunkiest thing since Mel Gibson and in would walk this weedy, middle-aged chap with glasses. I got a few shocks, I can tell you. And I expect other people were disappointed with me, too, although I tried to describe myself honestly.

61

## Making Gay Relationships Work

**Martin**: I wasn't disappointed when I met Jake. I didn't know what to expect and I hadn't built up a fantasy. I was glad that he'd seen my picture, then he couldn't say that I'd misled him. It was the first time I'd replied to an advert like that and I was a little nervous. But as soon as I met Jake in the pub, I relaxed and I knew we were going to get on. We've been together for eighteen months now, and it's still going strong. We're making plans to buy a house together.

There aren't any statistics about the success-rate of personal ads in the gay press, but their sheer number seems to indicate that they are - at the very least - a source of hope.

Often the ads are explicitly sexual and offer nothing more than "fun" (which is the favourite euphemism for sex in British gay personal ads). The law does not permit advertisers in Britain to be as explicit as their American counterparts. In papers such as "The Advocate", personal advertisers are often very precise about the type of sex they are seeking. In Britain a variety of code words and *doubles entendres* have to be employed to get the message over. This can make ads almost incomprehensible to the uninitiated.

However, more and more advertisers are stating that they are looking for a greater commitment. Expressions like "tired of the scene" and "ready for something more meaningful" are appearing with increasing frequency.

If you are thinking of placing an ad in search of a partner, make your intentions clear so that those who are seeking just a sexual encounter will not misunderstand you.

If, on the other hand, you are scanning the personals for suitable ads to respond to, you will probably realise that replying to ads that say: "Humpy, well-hung guy seeks others for occasional fun times" is unlikely to bring you in touch with someone who wants to settle into a lasting relationship.

One of the disadvantages of advertising in a national magazine is that you're likely to receive replies from people who are simply too far away to be able to make anything more than occasional contact. It is unlikely that a successful, long-term relationship can be sustained with someone several hundred miles away.

There has been some research into how relationships develop - including non-sexual relationships - and it confirms what most of us have discovered for ourselves: you are far more likely to have a satisfactory relationship with a neighbour or work colleague who you see most days than with, say, a pen-pal who lives on the other side of the country and who you see only once or twice a year. The same goes for deeper relationships; if your lover isn't easily available, then your relationship won't progress very far. It can be sustained for a while if there is the promise that you might be getting together more permanently, but it can never take the place of an on-the-spot lover who is easy to reach. It is important, therefore, when drafting an ad to specify where you live, and how far you are prepared to travel to meet people.

Being honest about your age, appearance and status is also important. It is possible to accentuate the positive without actually lying about the negative. Many gay men who aren't beautiful in the conventional sense compensate by developing charming, funny or assertive personalities. Play up the good points, but not to the extent that you are misleading potential respondents.

## Making Gay Relationships Work

Leave out of your ad any word that creates a negative or downbeat impression: "lonely", "depressed", "fed up", "unhappy", etc. That may be how you feel at the time, but it will deter partners from putting pen to paper. Think about the things that would attract you to a potential respondent and then include them; do you for instance value honesty, integrity, a sense of humour, affection, intelligence? Is social status important to you? Are you a fanatical vegetarian, non-smoker, socialist or Hindu? Do you like art or do you prefer football? Anything that is really important in your life should be included so that no-one gets the wrong impression.

Perhaps the most frequently-included phrase is "must be non-camp" or "non-effeminate" or "straight-acting". It means that gay men on the look-out for partners do not, in the main, rate effeminate men very highly, particularly not "screaming queens". However politically incorrect this might be, we have to accept that it is a fact of life. As a correspondent to one of Britain's gay newspapers wrote: "What makes us gay in the first place is the fact that we are attracted to the maleness of our partner, not to some parody of femaleness." This does not necessarily mean that those who are "effeminate" won't find a partner, some people go out of their way to find partners who *are* effeminate.

Try not to be too specific, particularly about the physical attributes of your potential partner. We all have to make allowances in the end: the perfect partner who fulfils all our requirements and gives us everything we want is likely to exist only in our fantasies.

Finally, do make an effort to reply to all the letters you receive. If someone has taken the trouble to write to you, however inappropriate they may seem, a brief reply telling them that you don't want to pursue their approach will save a lot of bad feeling. And please return any photographs sent to you - they can be an expensive item. These small courtesies can make a lot of difference to people of goodwill who are basically looking for the same thing you are.

## Telephone Dating Services

The gay press carries a lot of advertising from telephone dating agencies, which also might be worth a try. The idea is that you ring up a premium-rate number and listen to a selection of tape-recordings of men describing themselves and what they're looking for, in much the same way as they would in a personal ad. Each is given a code number and if you are interested, you ring another number to ask to be put in touch with the man or men of your choice. If you want your own message to be played on the line, then you ring the same number and record it. If you are planning to do this, then perhaps it's a good idea to write it out beforehand in case your mind goes blank when the recording begins.

These telephone services are becoming more and more sophisticated, and you can now access any calls which have been made in response to your ad by using a pin number. You need never speak to anyone directly at the company, it's all done by computer.

Naturally these services make their money from the length of time they keep you on the line, and it has been suggested that some of them actually make up messages or play out of date ones in order to keep callers listening as long as possible. It is difficult to know if you're being taken for a ride or not. You pays your money and you takes your chance. I have no idea of the success or otherwise of these lines - I have been unable to find anyone who admitted to using them. However, the fact that they continue to advertise extensively seems to indicate that something is happening to someone.

## Gay Groups

For those who aren't into the heavy competition of pubs and clubs and whose nerves won't stand the apprehension involved in blind dates, an answer might be a special interest gay group.

A glance at the listings in any gay magazine (*Gay Times* is the most complete) or a call to a Lesbian and Gay Switchboard will reveal a plethora of groups catering for all kinds of interests, from Giro users to nudists; from bridge players to rambling clubs. Others simply offer a variety of social activities. The advantage of these groups is that they provide members with a common interest and purpose, and a focus for socialising which doesn't necessitate devastating good looks or aggressive sexuality. You can get to know people while involved in activities which you all find interesting and which aren't necessarily sexual. These groups are a good way of making a circle of friends as well as looking for a partner. I joined a gay drama group in my youth which provided me with a lot of fun, an outlet for my creativity, a circle of enduring friends and eventually a partnership which lasted eleven years. I've joined many other groups since, and nearly all of them have provided me with something good in the way of human relationships.

For the shy person, such groups can provide an excellent gateway to gay life. They are non-threatening and often very welcoming and supportive. However, for the newcomer, a gay group that has a long-established membership may seem cliquey and unfriendly. Everyone seems to know each other and breaking into the circle seems impossible. For the first few visits, a new member can feel excluded or even rejected. My advice is to persevere until people get to know you. If you aren't very good at initiating conversations, or if your confidence has temporarily deserted you in this scary new environment, don't let it worry you too much. Believe it or not, most people feel that way: it's just that some are better than others at covering it up with a show of confidence. A number of groups I know have 'welcomers' to encourage new members and ensure they don't feel left out.

This was Gordon's experience when he joined his local gay social group:

> "I hated it at first. I thought: God, aren't they stuck up. Nobody spoke to me and I just sat in a corner and looked nervous. I nearly didn't go to the next meeting because I'd been so miserable at the first, but there was this speaker that interested me, so I forced myself to go. I didn't feel so bad the second time, and someone actually started a conversation with me. I didn't have the nerve to speak to anyone before they spoke to me, but once the ice was broken I opened up and started smiling, and this chap introduced me to some other people and it went on from there. I'm now secretary of the group and I love it."

Meeting a partner is often a matter of sheer good fortune, but hopefully these suggestions will help those who are engaged in the search to stack the odds a little more in their favour.

# Chapter Three:

# When to take the plunge

You've found the man with whom you feel you'd like to make a loving partnership. The sex is wonderful, you get on like a house on fire, have lots of fun and you agree on so many things. It all seems perfect - but when do you decide that the time has come to start regarding yourselves as a couple with special responsibilities for each other, and maybe even sharing a home?

It's an exciting time and one of immense joy, but scary, too. After all, it isn't every day that you embrace a completely new lifestyle and you are going to have to take some big risks. However long you hesitate, and however much thought you give to the matter, you can never be sure you are doing the right thing. Even if you think you've considered every eventuality—where you will live, how you will live, even down to who will do the washing up—things can still go wrong. This is not to say that careful preparation isn't important. It's certainly less likely that your relationship will run aground if you put in the spadework first. Even the best prepared can find that totally unforeseen problems will turn the relationship sour. As the gay writer Michael Carson said, homosexuals are people who "embark on a journey without maps - maps so readily doled out to heterosexuals".

## When Do We Move In Together?

As you get to know one another, and you recognise that you are moving towards a bigger commitment, you might consider living together. Don't be anxious to make the decision unless there is some urgent practical reason to do so. Give yourselves time to be sure that it's the right step for you both, for it is at this crucial point that you should review the many additional alternatives open to gay couples.

It is quite possible, for instance, for two people to have a satisfactory relationship without actually living under the same roof. A lot of gay partners have continued to live separately in their own homes, while still considering themselves to be a couple. Writing in a pamphlet from the Lesbian and Gay Christian Movement ("Exploring Lifestyles"- GCM), Malcolm Johnson said:

"An old closeted cleric said to me recently, 'I never met a homosexual couple who have been together for more than a year. It can't last.' I had news for him. It made me go home and write down the names of 92 couples I know personally. 35 had been together up to three years, 34 between four and eight years and 23 over nine years. Interestingly enough, 23 of these couples did not live together - a smaller percentage than in the

American study where 44 per cent of male couples did not share a home. There is an obvious difference from the heterosexual world. The reasons may be that jobs conflict. Of the 21 clergy in my sample only nine live with their lover. Or perhaps age and demanding parents do not understand the situation. 'Richard's mother doesn't understand, if I lived with them I'd throttle her. He's unlikely to kick her out, so we'll never live together until she dies.' And some gays feel that living apart accords more with the lifestyle they wish to adopt."

The living apart set-up seems to suit some people, and it certainly has much to recommend it. Of the couples I met who live like this, many have an arrangement whereby they stay over at one of their houses on several evenings of the week, and at weekends. Some nights they spend on their own, or with other people.

The credit side of this arrangement is that if you are planning to keep your relationship 'discreet' (or even completely in the closet), it's the easiest way to do it. There is little doubt that if two men over the age of twenty-five move in together, it won't be long before the neighbours, friends and family begin to speculate about the nature of the cohabitation. If you live separately from your partner, you might never be linked in such a way. Keeping independent abodes also means you are spared most of the hassles which go with sharing a home. If you're getting on each other's nerves, you can simply go back to your own houses. It also means that you keep total independence in many other ways: perhaps there will be the opportunity for other sexual relationships which can be conducted with less friction in your own home; you can keep your finances separate, too. You will be master of your own territory. This is all fine if you have the resources to do it, but keeping two homes going when you can manage with one is an enormous expense. It's all a matter of personal priorities.

There is a debit side, too. If you are living apart in order not to be 'found out', you are devaluing your relationship by denying its existence to important people in your lives. We will return to the effects of keeping your relationship secret in Chapter Six.

Living apart also means that you miss out on the enriching experience of living together. Domesticity and a shared home can bring a thousand and one simple joys as well as frustrations. The joint struggles which might have tested and strengthened your relationship will be diluted by you ability to walk away from them.

## Opposites Don't Necessarily Attract

Despite what you might have heard about opposites attracting, it ain't necessarily so in human relationships. Research has shown that the more a couple have in common, the better their long-term chances of staying together. This is not to say that partners have to agree on absolutely everything in order to succeed. Indeed, it would probably be a very bland and boring relationship that didn't have some areas of disagreement. What would you have to talk about? What could you teach each other? But while small differences can be stimulating, other areas are so irreconcilable that they are bound to lead to big problems later in the relationship.

Some psychologists argue that the essential difference or 'tension' which creates mystery and interest in a male-female relationship is absent from a relationship between members of the same sex, and in order to attain that 'tension' of discovery and curiosity, it is important that male couples still have plenty to find out about each other. It could be argued, of course, that the 'tension' that makes male-female relationships interesting also makes them fragile. The repeated complaint of straight men is that they 'don't understand' their wives or girlfriends, and although some men love trying to solve the mystery of the opposite sex, others are irritated by it and spend as much time away from their women-folk as they can. A visit to any straight pub in the country (any pub aimed at the over thirties, that is) will illustrate this lack of understanding between men and women. The men socialise together and the women - if they are present at all - will seek each other out for a 'better quality' of chat. Many straight men will admit that they don't actually have any women *friends* (as opposed to lovers), and that they have nothing to talk about with women. Similarly straight women will tell you that if they want a 'proper conversation' they have to turn to their women friends to find it. Maybe the 'tension' between men and women rapidly loses its fascination for some people and turns into an irritation. This might also go some way to explaining why a surprising number of straight women have a gay man as their best friend. They get a male perspective without the 'tension' that goes with their relationships with straight men.

Bringing different skills and strengths to the relationship in a way that complements and supports the partnership is quite different to being fundamentally at odds over issues of personal morality and ethical values. I would say, for instance, that a relationship between a born-again Christian and an aggressive atheist is hardly likely to survive for very long, nor is a relationship between a true blue Tory and a member of the Socialist Workers Party. It is no use hoping that your partner's deeply-held principles will change (or that you will be able to change them) once the relationship has become established. There are some issues that aren't negotiable. It is unfair to expect your partner to compromise beliefs that are important to him in order to fit in with your thinking. The points of contention will soon become apparent, and if these are matters that are intensely important to you, you should stop and ask whether you can accept these different political, religious or ethical values in your partner.

Melvyn and Robin had been 'courting' for several months, and had enjoyed a passionate fun-loving time. Melvyn was a committed socialist, profoundly concerned with the political situation and with the promotion of his chosen party. Robin, on the other hand, had little interest in politics - what interest he did have seemed to lean slightly to the right of centre, something which he had inherited from his parents. He was amused at first by Melvyn's intensity during political conversations with friends. He found it difficult to understand his lover's deep convictions, but indulged him.

When they decided that the time was approaching for them to set up home together, Robin suggested that they accept his father's offer of money to buy a flat. Robin's father had made his fortune from property speculation - a form of activity which Melvyn considered 'parasitic'. He pointedly refused to accept any money from Robin's father, and said he would prefer that they manage on their own. Robin was totally bemused by this attitude; he realised that if they were obliged to manage on their own money, they would be forced to live in modest, if not squalid, accommodation - at least for a while. It was at this point that Robin recognised that the political differences could no longer be ignored, they had become a major barrier between them. It was soon apparent that Melvyn was not joking, and that he would not compromise his beliefs for the sake of convenience. Robin, on the other hand, didn't feel strongly about anything that didn't directly affect him and had imagined that given time, Melvyn would come round to accepting his point of view.

It was soon clear that not only would Robin become seriously annoyed by Melvyn's uncompromising stance, Melvyn would, in turn, feel frustrated by Robin's apparent lack of interest in what he saw as political justice. They decided not to move in together until they discovered just how intractable their problem would turn out to be.

They remained friendly, and continued to have good sex for some time. Eventually, however, they came to realise that more than sex and dancing were needed to sustain their relationship. They began to drift apart and eventually decided to call it a day. It was not a bitter parting, and when their paths cross they still get a certain pleasure from each other. But they are also grateful that they didn't make any hasty decisions about rearranging their lives.

## Age and Racial Considerations

Other fundamental differences between partners can also weigh the relationship down. Significant age differences can be a particular stumbling block. The odds seemed stacked against the long-term survival of a relationship in which partners are a generation apart. Not only will there be an inevitable difference in attitudes and needs, there will be significant discrepancies in priorities, energy and maybe financial resources. When Project Sigma asked 930 gay men 'What do you look for in a sexual partner?', 21% mentioned the age of the partner. Those who specified a partner older than themselves had a mean age of 25 years, those specifying a partner of a similar age had a mean age of 32 years, and those specifying a younger partner had a mean age of 43 years. Just over 43% of the couples interviewed were within five years of each other, although the biggest age difference in the study was fifty-three years.

However, the younger man might be finding his feet and the company of an older man can provide reassurance at such a time; many a young man has found a father figure to help him through this critical stage of adjustment. And many an older gay man has discovered the joy of having a younger person around to share and benefit from his experience. There is nothing wrong with such arrangements, and there are glowing examples of them succeeding in some form over long periods.

But the younger partner is likely to change and broaden his horizons at a much faster rate than his partner. What is fresh and exciting to a young people is possibly old-hat to the next generation. Quite often, in these circumstances, an agreement is reached between the partners that satisfies both of them and allows the relationship to survive. Harold and Tim are one such couple. Tim is a vibrant twenty-five year old, very much involved in his career and ambitious to progress. He met Harold who is thirty years his senior at a disco, and they found they had a lot in common. Harold has already had a successful career in the field that Tim has chosen (accountancy), and so they have much to talk about. Harold feels he can help Tim avoid some of the mistakes he has made himself during his own career. Tim respects and values Harold's experience, gratefully receiving his guidance and making full use of it. In return, Tim gives Harold the comfort and companionship that he wants, and both partners are satisfied with the arrangement.

At the beginning of their relationship, their sex life had been warm and exciting, as Harold explains:

"It was like a new lease of life for me, a second chance. I had all the old familiar feelings: walking on air, increased libido, wanting to be with him every minute of the day, and that sort of thing. But there was always the thought in the back of my mind that he would soon get tired of me and move on. I just lived from day to day. But we seemed to keep going and the relationship got stronger. I think I was the first to start cooling down, having been in a relationship before I knew that the excitement would eventually wear off, and I wasn't overly worried when it did. But Tim was still romantic even after a couple of years, which was very nice. We've been together almost five years now, and looking back I can see the enormous changes that have come about. Tim spends much more time with other people than he did when we were first together, and I don't mind that at all because I have my own circle. I know he has sex outside of our relationship, and I don't mind that either, so long as he takes precautions. I trust him to be sensible - I know him well enough to be sure that he isn't taking silly risks. And I don't feel jealous about it, even though I thought I would. I don't want sex as much as he does, so what right have I to deny him his chances? The sexual element of our partnership now seems far less important than our home life. Tim always comes home to me in the end, however bound up he might become in other relationships. I feel we are pretty stable as a couple, but I don't take anything for granted. After all, he is still a relatively young man and I'm well into middle-age now. I feel the only thing that could cause us to split up is if a younger man comes along who Tim falls in love with."

Partners from different races will also find extra problems, but if they are basically of similar outlook, age and desire, their relationship has every chance of being successful. Any problems of racism which might be experienced by each partner as they move from one culture to another can be endured with mutual support. Such pressure, if it is handled constructively, can actually increase the will to survive. Those from cultures in which homosexuality is totally unacceptable may find they have a double problem of rejection from their own culture and racism from the majority culture in which they are now forced to live. Groups who will support those who are having these kinds of difficulties are listed in the back of this book.

The trick is spotting which of the differences between you are so fundamental that they are totally irreconcilable, and which will be complementary and add another dimension to your relationship. If one partner is very practically-minded, while the other has an imaginative, abstract approach to life, there is room for mutual growth. What the practical partner lacks in imagination his lover can make up for, and vice versa. Each can gain from the other's special qualities in these instances, and both can grow as a consequence. There is no fundamental disagreement here, simply an admiration and acceptance of each other's positive qualities.

## The HIV Dilemma

Your new relationship may bring you a dilemma which previous generations have not had to face: the issue of the Human Immunodeficiency Virus, thought to be the organism which can lead to the development of Aids. You will probably know quite a lot about HIV, how it is spread and what to do to avoid infection - and if you don't, you have a bounden duty to find out.

The question is, can you both be certain that you haven't come into contact with the virus at some time in the past? This means that one of the first conversations you must have together is about your health status and, if it is unknown, about previous lives. Both of you must assess honestly whether it is possible that you have come into contact with HIV. If there is the smallest possibility, then you must stick to safer sex practices. However enamoured you are of your new partner, you must not be tempted to have unprotected sex until you are both confident that neither of you is infected with HIV.

Unless both of you are absolutely certain of your present antibody status (whether you have antibodies to HIV in your bloodstream), you are faced with the dilemma of whether or not to take the antibody test.

The advantage of both of you taking the test (in fact it would require several tests over a long period to be certain) is that if you were negative you would be able to forget safer sex guidelines when you were together and so long as you remained faithful to each other. Neither of you need be stressed by the worries and suspicions which night arise. If it turned out that either of you were HIV positive, you could take steps to ensure that you protected your health as much as possible, change your diet and lifestyle to make the development of HIV-related illnesses less likely.

The disadvantages are that if you took the test there could be no guarantee of absolute confidentiality. Even if the test proved negative, simply taking it can have dire consequences for employment, accommodation, insurance, mortgages and so on, although efforts are being made to limit this. If one of you were positive, how would he cope with the news? And would your love and commitment to each other be strong enough to see you through, or would it be the end of the road?

I suggest most strongly that, before you make any decisions, you talk the whole thing over with a counsellor from one of the agencies specialising in Aids advice. The Terrence Higgins Trust is familiar with the situation and will help you work through it until you have come to a conclusion about what is best for you. In the meantime, remember that safer sex doesn't have to be boring; it has the potential to take you to the limits of erotic excitement if enough imagination is employed.

There is a potential pitfall here; Aids educators and 'moralists' have been saying for some time that if gay men were to embark upon stable, monogamous relationships, their chances of encountering HIV would be much reduced or eliminated. This argument has flaws, however. Human relationships cannot be sustained simply as a convenient means of avoiding disease. If partners are staying in a relationship which has no meaning for them simply as a precaution, then they are asking for emotional problems - possibly quite severe ones. And as we've already said, there can be no guarantees that one or both of the partners isn't already carrying the virus anyway. The idea that monogamy can protect you from HIV is appealing, but shouldn't lull you into a false sense of security or into accepting a potentially misery-inducing relationship.

Some recent research (Project Sigma, reported in *Capital Gay*) indicates that once gay men enter a relationship they begin to abandon safer sex practices with their partner. Of the men in regular relationships who took part in the survey, only 37% used a condom while being fucked, and only 34% taking the active role used one. This seems to suggest that partners who have made a commitment to each other either want to demonstrate their trust by abandoning safer sex or, perhaps, they simply become complacent.

## What Do You Want?

Do you have a firm idea in your mind of the kind of relationship that you want and how it will develop? Most people would answer that by saying that they want that 'special someone' as a partner, and a big romance to form the overture to a fulfilling long-term commitment. The obvious things that such a partner will provide include: companionship, love, mutual support and shared expenses. This remains the ultimate ideal for most of us (although not always at the same stage in our lives), but the pitfalls between wishes and reality are numerous.

You need to ask yourself: is the happy-ever-after dream of a full-time, long-term relationship, complete with all its restrictions, really what I want? Am I ready to put in the work that is undoubtedly needed to make the relationship succeed? Is this the right time to embark on creating such a lifestyle or do I have other things to achieve, different roads to travel that can best be travelled alone?

The whole purpose of changing your life in such a fundamental way is to improve it. Ask yourself: will the quality of my life be significantly enhanced if I give up my single status and take on a partner? If there is any doubt in your mind, make a list of the advantages and disadvantages. Don't worry if it all seems cold and calculating, it will simply help get things clear in your mind.

It's amazing how many people fall into the trap of imagining that because everyone says that one-to-one relationships are the "done thing" or the "mature culmination" and so on, they are automatically correct. The truth is, you don't *have* to opt for coupledom just because most people think you should. And it is here that gay people have another significant advantage over heterosexuals. In the straight world there are a thousand and one expectations loaded on to the shoulders of each individual: it is taken for granted that everyone will marry at some point in their life, and have children. Only a minority of straight people seem to argue with this notion. Heterosexuals who never marry at any stage in their life are a rarity. Such is the stampede to enter into matrimony and such is the social pressure (or maybe the intrinsic appeal of the institution) that many gay people get caught up in it, too.

The reason gay men get married to heterosexual women are many and varied. For some it is a desire to conform and not to be regarded as an outcast or maybe to fulfil the expectations of the family; for others it is simply a desire to have children and raise a family. Some might enter marriage as an attempt to escape the truth of their sexual orientation and yet others will use it as a cover-up, leading a double life. Few of the gay people who go into marriage can totally abandon their true sexuality, and many gay-straight

81

marriages fail because of the pressure created by trying to deny something so fundamental.

It becomes clear from the divorce statistics that pair-bonding is not a panacea. If you are lonely, insecure or feel maladjusted in some way, then finding a partner who will love and cherish you might seem to offer a solution to all your problems. Some individuals have, indeed, found a new way of living inside a relationship which has solved many of the problems which plagued them before; others have loaded their partners with unbearably heavy expectations. It is unreasonable to think that a lover will be able to solve any deeply-rooted psychological problem for you. If you are, for instance, addicted to alcohol or drugs, you cannot reasonably expect your partner to provide the "answer" to your problem - although he might. You will, however, be more likely to be disappointed if you enter into a relationship with such expectations. Your partner will probably feel abused because you will end up blaming him for something that is basically your problem.

Hang-ups, failings, imperfections - this is the emotional baggage that we all carry, and which we take with us into our relationships. If you have big problems, face up to them and talk them through honestly. If he loves you, your partner will probably want to support you and help you sort them out. If you love him, you'll resist the temptation to say: "It's all your fault - being with you has made it worse."

However, taking on a lover with problems doesn't mean you can't ever cut your losses when you recognise that even after you've done your best, you've bitten off more than you can chew. If you can't cope, you will have every right to distance yourself from problems which are beyond you. You will probably feel guilty about abandoning someone

82

who is already distressed, but sometimes it can't be avoided. That's one of the risks that partners must face when they set out together.

This was the case with Rick who found, after many years of living with Patrick, that the prospect of a lifetime battling against Pat's drink problem was more than he could take.

"I knew Pat had a problem with drink, but for the first few years it seemed to be under control. Whenever we socialised in the pub - it was always in the pub - he would come home plastered. I put this down to high spirits, he had just got carried away with the atmosphere. But then he started drinking at home. I would sometimes come home from work to find him crashed out on the settee, totally out of his head on booze. Then he started to stay out at night, and would come home next day looking like hell. I wasn't worried that he was seeing someone else. It was obvious that he had simply been out drinking somewhere. If I tried to raise the issue with him when he was sober, he would say 'Yes, I know I've got a problem', but if I said anything when he was drunk, he would get abusive and threatening. Life for us was becoming very narrow and restricted. If we weren't going to the pub, we weren't going anywhere.

I went to a group for the families of alcoholics and found out how other people were coping - mainly by denying that they couldn't cope any more. It took a long time for me to come to the realisation that Pat's drinking was destroying my life as well as his own. I had to get away from it."

If both partners are willing to accept responsibility for their own actions, their own feelings and their own problems, then they can also work together at coming to terms with them. Hopefully this book will give you some guidelines for doing this creatively and with love.

## Living Together

According to Project Sigma, 22% of the men who considered themselves to be in a regular relationship lived together. If you want to move in with your partner, it might be an easy process - one of you will be well-established in a house or flat with plenty of spare room, and the other simply moves in. However, if both of you are well-established and both have room for the other, you will have to work out which home would be most sensible to share. An alternative is to start together in a completely new dwelling. This has the added advantage of being neither partner's former exclusive territory. You might even decide to keep both houses going until you are certain you've done the right thing.

You also need to consider which is the best location for both of your jobs. Is one of you going to have to move from one part of the country to another? Will one of you have to give up or change your job so that you can be together?

Sometimes it seems that one partner is taking all the risks: uprooting, relocating, giving up an established home, finding a new job, leaving family and friends. To give up everything that is familiar and secure and plunge into a completely new, untried life takes a lot of courage. Even if it isn't one-sided, there will still be a desire to be as sure as possible that the whole thing has a reasonable chance of

Gay Christian Movement can give you ideas and contacts. As they say:

> "Just as there is no such thing as Christian Marriage, so there are no Christian Gay Unions. There is marriage, there is gay union. Christian gay unions have a different direction and perspective; there is a Christian approach and interpretation of the union, and organisations like the Lesbian and Gay Christian Movement exist to help a couple discover what these are. Gay Switchboard now has at least one enquiry a week concerning Exchange of Vows and numbers are sure to increase. Some Anglican and Free Church clergy are now ready to discuss the subject with a couple but our unsympathetic hierarchy forces secrecy. The Metropolitan Community Church can, of course, be more open. Couples ask for different things; so the service can be constructed around their wishes. Those who have been together for years want to stress thanksgiving (in a Eucharist perhaps), others want a house blessing. At present more women than men, more working class than others are coming forward. A wise priest will want to see a couple several times to discuss their hopes, their background and Christian commitment, and look to see if they are using him to prop up and ailing relationship. Some may have to wait as, unlike heterosexuals, there is usually no 'engagement' to test sincerity."

If you are atheist, agnostic or simply uncomfortable with religious rites, you can still mark the beginning of your

## Making Gay Relationships Work

Some couples are even opting for individually drawn up contracts tailored to their own needs. This is particularly true in America where some straight couples have drawn up marriage contracts to include such promises as never to smoke, never to get fat and never to demand that the wife has children. Some have drawn up contracts for a fixed term, say five years, which are renewable or renegotiable after that time. Some have agreed that their relationship will not be sexually exclusive.

It might seem cold-blooded to draw up such a contract at the beginning of a partnership, when romance is still very much the order of the day. Indeed, you might feel that you can draw up more realistic guidelines when you have been together a bit longer and are more aware of the issues which might need formalising.

For most gay couples there is no need for a formalised contract, they just make up the rules as they go along. A developing relationship is in constant flux and so there should be plenty of flexibility for change as circumstances alter. The trouble is that many people make assumptions about their partner's attitudes based on wishful thinking rather than reality. When the partner fails to behave in the manner which the other partner assumed he would, conflict arises. This is a communication problem which can be overcome.

A contract between a gay couple is normally simply an agreement - written down if you want to give it an air of formality, although it will have no force in law. A promise by two men to be faithful to each other would not hold water in court, but other things - particularly related to finances - can be made legally binding. There is no doubt that all gay couples must make wills if they wish their money and property to go to each other. If you enter into joint financial commitments, you should make legally binding arrangements to cover all eventualities. You should nominate each other as next of kin. All these issues should be sorted out by a qualified legal adviser. If you are making wills, it is far better to give the job to a solicitor than to try and do it yourself. If everything is straightforward and simple you might be able to manage on your own with a form from the stationers, but there are so many possible complications that the investment in legal advice is a sensible one. A few pounds spent at this stage could save a small fortune in legal fees should a will be contested by relatives. Shop around and ask solicitors what they charge for drawing up wills—there can be a significant price difference between one firm and another. Gay solicitors with specialised knowledge and sympathy for your concerns can be found advertising in the gay press.

If you are sharing a home you should make some sort of mutual commitment. Should one of you be giving up his home to live with the other, you might like to make some arrangement that wouldn't leave one of you homeless and penniless should it all go wrong. Discuss such arrangements with your solicitor.

If you are living in rented accommodation, make sure you have equal tenancy rights if possible. If you are living in local authority accommodation, then find out the council's policy on passing tenancy from one person to another. If the flat is only in one name, and the named person dies, his gay partner can be evicted, although this policy is being reviewed. A few local authorities are amending their policies to cover this eventuality, but not all of them. Ask at the housing department or at the Housing Advice Centre if you are in doubt.

## Pets Are Valuable

A large number of gay couples introduce pets into their homes. Whether this is as a child substitute - as so many suggest - doesn't really matter. There is little doubt that pets can play a central role in binding a couple together. The lesbian fondness for cats is well documented and has become something of a joke in the gay community. I know several gay couples for whom a dog or cat plays a central role in their life together. If the presence of a dog or cat or parrot or goldfish makes home feel more like home, then that can be nothing but good. And pets can often provide a focus that takes the heat out of a partnership that is becoming too intense.

## Ceremony And Ritual

Certain people—mainly inspired by rigid religious dogma—have tried to narrow down the meaning of "family" so as to exclude anyone who is not married and not heterosexual. This attempt by fanatical traditionalists to hijack the sense of "family" for their own exclusive use is irritating but, in the end, meaningless. We can all create our own family in whatever way we choose, and there is little they can do to stop us. Let them label our partnerships "pretend" if they want to - we know there is nothing pretend about the love we feel for each other, and nobody can take that away from us.

What you cannot do as a gay couple is to have a wedding ceremony that will have any legal meaning. If religious belief is important to you, and you feel you would like your relationship to have a formal blessing, then there are priests who will perform this for you. The Lesbian and

Gay Christian Movement can give you ideas and contacts. As they say:

"Just as there is no such thing as Christian Marriage, so there are no Christian Gay Unions. There is marriage, there is gay union. Christian gay unions have a different direction and perspective; there is a Christian approach and interpretation of the union, and organisations like the Lesbian and Gay Christian Movement exist to help a couple discover what these are. Gay Switchboard now has at least one enquiry a week concerning Exchange of Vows and numbers are sure to increase. Some Anglican and Free Church clergy are now ready to discuss the subject with a couple but our unsympathetic hierarchy forces secrecy. The Metropolitan Community Church can, of course, be more open. Couples ask for different things; so the service can be constructed around their wishes. Those who have been together for years want to stress thanksgiving (in a Eucharist perhaps), others want a house blessing. At present more women than men, more working class than others are coming forward. A wise priest will want to see a couple several times to discuss their hopes, their background and Christian commitment, and look to see if they are using him to prop up and ailing relationship. Some may have to wait as, unlike heterosexuals, there is usually no 'engagement' to test sincerity."

If you are atheist, agnostic or simply uncomfortable with religious rites, you can still mark the beginning of your partnership in some kind of ceremonial way. An example of the Gay and Lesbian Humanist Association's "affirmation ceremony", is reproduced here. The Association (see Listings at the back of the book) can provide an experienced officiant to conduct the ceremony or you could ask a friend or relative. The ceremony is a fairly simple one; it contains some poetry, mutual pledges and an exchange of rings, and it an be adapted according to people's wishes. It can be held in the couple's home or in some public place such as a lesbian and gay centre or a gay pub or club. It can be completely private or (more usually) with friends present as witnesses, and followed by a party or reception.

The Gay and Lesbian Humanists suggest following the text below - with a suitable selection of music and, if desired, a different poetry selection. The ceremony is, of course, non-religious and has no legal status:

## THE ENTRY (with music)

In most cases it will be the custom for those present to be assembled in the room prior to the couple's arrival. The officiant can either stand near the entrance to meet the couple or stand at a suitable place in the room and allow the couple to approach. Once the music has stopped, the officiant makes a short opening statement, asking those present to be seated, welcoming them and explaining that the couple (giving their names) have invited their friends (and perhaps family) to witness their commitment to each other.

## The Affirmation

The Officiant invites the couple to stand with him. He invites the friends to either sit or gather round the couple, whichever seems appropriate. He starts the ceremony by saying: "We have come together to witness the joining together of two lives. In the words of Shakespeare's sonnet:

"Let me not the marriage of true minds
Admit impediments, Love is not Love
Which alters when alterations finds,
Or bends with the remover to remove:
O, No! - it is an ever-fixed mark,
That looks upon tempests and is never shaken.
It is the start to every wandering barque,
Whose worth's unknown, although it's height be taken.
Love's not Time's fool, though rosy lips and cheeks
Within his bending sickle's compass come;
Love alters not with the brief hours and weeks,
But bears it out even on the edge of doom.
If this be error, and upon me proved,
I never write, nor no man ever loved."

**Officiant**: (name) and (name) have come here in affection and honour to say before us that they will henceforth share their home, and combine in mutual living and responsibility. Love is the wish of the whole self to unite with another to the end of personal completeness. Touched by this love, nature yields tenderness, togetherness, simplicity, honesty and delight. When two people honestly and sincerely declare their affection for each other, they are affirming the precious truth that love is the foundation of all life - between two people, between friends, between all humanity. Now, (addressing the couple) will you join your right hands. Do you aspire to love each other and to live together in a spirit of tolerance, mutual support, and concern for each other's well being, sharing your responsibilities, your problems and your joys?

**Couple**: Yes, we do.

**Officiant**: I now ask both of you to speak in truth to each other and to repeat in the spirit of faithful engagement these words of solemn declaration that voluntarily bind you together. Will you (name) say after me: "I want it to be known / that I (name) / take you (name) / to be my lover / and promise to cherish, love and comfort you / for all my life / I offer you this ring / as a symbol of my love."

Now the two of you together, repeat after me these words: "We have openly declared our love for each other / and do pledge ourselves / to prefer each other's good / from this day forward / and to love and to cherish / in sickness and in health / as long as we may live."

And now we offer to you (name) our sincere good wishes. May you have joy and give joy and make your home a source of strength and happiness to yourself and others. You may now kiss each other."
**THE EXIT (with music)."**

If you decide to have a ritual of any kind to mark your love, then why not make it an occasion for real celebration? Not everyone will be able to invite their family and work colleagues and not everyone will want to, but if you are going to the trouble of arranging a ceremony, part of it will be to validate your partnership in the eyes of those who are important to you. In a way it is saying: We take this relationship seriously and we want you to take it seriously, too. If you decide that you'd like to have such an occasion make sure it is joyous and happy as well as serious and solemn.

# Chapter Four:

# The ground rules

The three essential elements needed to create a successful relationship are trust, respect and acceptance; without these nothing else is possible. But, you might ask, what do such abstract concepts mean? How adaptable are they? And do they mean the same thing to everyone? I suggest you read this chapter together with your partner and then discuss your feelings about these issues.

Many couples think that these precious gifts flow automatically from "being in love" but, as many have discovered to their cost, that isn't always true. One partner might try to control the other, using many different methods: guilt, money, violence, humiliation. One partner may try to ensure that his interests take preference over those of his lover. Maybe these ploys are used unconsciously, but that doesn't make them any the less harmful. If such manipulations form part of your relationship, then one or more of the three cornerstones of trust, respect and acceptance is missing. So let us look more closely at these three indispensable ingredients.

## Trust

Trust is being confident that your partner means what he says. If he makes a promise you can be sure that he means to keep it; if he makes a commitment you are sure that he'll do his best to see it through. If you don't have trust then the relationship is almost certainly doomed. If you cannot depend on your partner honouring agreements that you have made together, then where are you? If promises that seem to be made in all good faith leave you feeling doubtful and vulnerable, what value do they have? If you cannot rest because somewhere along the line you do not believe what your partner has told you, then you will soon become tired of the arrangement.

On the other hand, if you know you can trust your partner to mean what he says then you can relax and enjoy each other. If he promises to be home in time for a long-arranged social event, and he is there at the appointed hour, then you don't have to worry; there doesn't have to be a confrontation, explanation and resentment. If he tells you that he's working late at the office, and you know that if you ring him there you'll find it's true, then that's fine. But if he tells you that he has to go away for the weekend on business and you subsequently discover that it had nothing to do with work, then there will come a stage when you will doubt everything he says. When partners routinely lie to each other, and when nothing can be wholeheartedly believed, the end is almost certainly in sight.

But let's be realistic: there probably isn't a relationship anywhere in the world that doesn't involve some kind of deception at times. Every couple will have its secrets, both from the world and from each other. In some ways it is not desirable to share absolutely everything with your partner - there have to be some things which you can totally call your own. The occasional little white lie can save hurt feelings and unnecessary worry, so long as they are kept to a minimum. Habitual lying will undermine the relationship, its inevitable escalation will result in neither partner knowing where they stand. No-one wants to feel that their most precious relationship is a source of doubt and suspicion.

Two people living together in close proximity cannot successfully lie to each other over an extended period, anyway. It's amazing how obvious to a live-in partner little changes of attitude can be. Small alterations in routine can become very obvious signals to a lover who probably knows you better than anyone in the world. Listen to this, from one gay man who had been in a partnership for many years:

"Nigel never worked late at his job. He always left at the same time and came straight home: he said he couldn't wait to get away. Then he suddenly started to stay on in the evening to 'sort things out' as he put it. The first few times he said it I thought it might be true and gave him the benefit of the doubt. But after the second week I began to realise that it didn't square with what had gone before. I challenged him about it and he admitted he was seeing someone else. I'd had my suspicions since the first day he announced he had to stay late at work. You just sort of know when something like that isn't true. we're trying to sort it our between us. I'm not sure what upset me most - his affair or his blatant lying to me."

Trust is one of the linchpins of a healthily functioning relationship - without it so many other things can't happen. But trust must be earned, and it often takes several years before partners truly and unreservedly come to trust each other.

## Respect

Respect is another essential element; if it is absent the partnership will soon be in deep water. If your partner feels you don't really respect his opinions, his achievements or his feelings, then you are in trouble. And this, like all the other things in your relationship, should be a two-way traffic; both must be able to look with pride at their partner and say: "Yes, you've done well. I'm proud of you." If you rejoice in your partner's achievements, then he will feel good and so will you. If you get a genuine sense of commitment from your partner, then you will feel good about yourself and your relationship. One of the things that most of us want from a loving partnership is a sense that someone will listen to what we say and respect it. It isn't necessary to agree about everything all the time, but differences of opinion should be afforded due dignity and consideration. If you feel safe to open your heart to your partner in the full knowledge that you are not going to be ridiculed or humiliated, then you have a precious gift.

However, if you want respect from your partner, then you must return the compliment. Your partner must be sure that if he achieves something he has worked for, you will be at his side sharing his triumph. And if he takes the risk of revealing his deepest yearnings, then he expects you to listen with sympathy.

Respect is such an important aspect of a relationship that it cannot be over-emphasised. Partners who don't respect each other are soon painfully apparent. They will criticise each other in company, ruthlessly using confidences to score points. This is not good; much of your relationship will be stamped 'private', to be kept between the two of you. Partners should be able to be confident that their mistakes and disappointments will not be used against them at the next dinner party.

It might even be worthwhile for both partners to make a pact near the beginning of their relationship (or now if the relationship is already established) to respect each other. Among the things to promise each other could be:

- Partners will make the best endeavour to support each other during difficult times.

- Partners will celebrate each other's success. Any element of competition which might exist between you must never tempt you to undermine or belittle your partner's efforts. If resentment and jealousy about differing scales of achievement begin to surface, then it is a serious problem and one which must be faced and resolved.

- Partners will be generous with their listening time. If one partner needs a sympathetic ear, then it should be given unstintingly.

- Some things in the relationship must be deemed private and not for public view. Both partners promise not to use personal failures or weaknesses as a weapon against the other. You should resist the temptation to score points against each other when in company - this might prove humiliating to one partner, and can rapidly get out of control.

Without respect it is impossible to conduct successful negotiations. If you do not respect your partner's opinions and do not regard his needs as important, then there can be no fair negotiation. If you imagine that your partner's needs are always to be placed second to your own, then you do not have respect for him and your relationship will be unbalanced and unjust. It is not likely that your partner will be happy in such a situation, and if he isn't happy, then you cannot get the most from your life together.

I see a distressing number of couples who routinely do not respect each other's dignity. Trying to humiliate a partner in public is a vicious and violent thing to do. Not only does it hurt him, it also causes pain and embarrassment for those who have to witness it. Ultimately it does nothing for the happiness of the aggressor, either. You may be angry or frustrated by what your partner is doing or saying, but there are other ways to express that anger than in cruelty and disrespect.

The ultimate disrespect, of course, expresses itself in physical violence. Research into gay relationships is revealing that physical abuse is more common than previously imagined. Using superior strength to control a partner or to punish him for not doing everything in the way that the other partner wants is totally unacceptable. Violent arguments might well develop into physical attacks, as can pent up frustration caused by the inability to communicate properly. Alcohol is frequently a factor.

Michael lived for many years in such an abusive relationship.

"It mostly happened when he was drunk - the rest of the time he restricted his abuse to the verbal variety. But if he'd had a few he became very aggressive. He would pick arguments and fights. Whatever I said he would twist it round so that he could argue with it. Whenever he got like this I would try to leave the room because I knew where it was leading, but he wouldn't let up until he'd got into such a frenzy that he would smack me. He was much stronger than I was, so there was little point in my fighting back - it would just have resulted in him hitting me more and getting even angrier. I put up with it for nearly ten years, because I loved him and also because I was afraid of what would happen if I walked out. I didn't really have anywhere else to go. Eventually I met someone else who saw what was going on in the relationship and persuaded me to get out before I was really injured.

I still think about him a lot and wish that it hadn't been that way, but I really did have to get away or one day he might have completely lost control and killed me.

The awful thing was that he didn't hate me. He always apologised when he was sober and told me that I was the most important person in the world for him. So why did he have so much anger?"

If your relationship is an abusive one - either physically or verbally - find some help. Call one of the gay helplines and discuss it with a counsellor there. Often it is difficult to see from the inside what is really happening and what the true options are.

## Acceptance

Acceptance is the third important element of a successful relationship: the acceptance that we are all imperfect. Just as you have to accept that you are not without fault, so you must accept that you partner is not perfect, either. Only when you have accepted and recognised each other's shortcomings can you progress.

This is not to say that faults which are causing serious difficulties between you should not be confronted and challenged, but having faults is not the same as being a faulty person. Each partner must recognise the impossibility of the other being without a single flaw. Sometimes these imperfections are temporary, sometimes they are intrinsic parts of our character. Sometimes they can be modified, sometimes they can't.

It may be, for instance, that your partner enjoys rather spiteful gossip while you deplore such an activity. Your partner listens with respect to your disapproval, but continues to gossip. Your option is to say: "When you and Glen get together and start criticising people and gossiping about them, it can be really quite cruel and malicious," or to say "You are a malicious and cruel person because you 'dish' your friends behind their back."

It's highly unlikely you would have made a full-scale commitment to someone who is intrinsically malicious and cruel. The truth is that you perceive a fault in your partner: he enjoys gossip. It's now up to you to accept and forgive that small vice without taking the leap into branding him a bad person.

You, on the other hand, might consider housework to be a trivial pursuit and put off doing cleaning jobs you've agreed to undertake. You may not be offended by an untidy house or an unhygienic kitchen, whereas your partner might be depressed by living in what he sees as "a pigsty". He considers your sluttishness to be a fault. He knows he'll never get you interested in cleaning and tidying however hard he tries. So now he has to accept that you have a different idea about household cleanliness. Your approach, as far as he is concerned, is imperfect. Once you unburden yourself of the need to try changing your partner's every imperfection, then you will find things move more smoothly. (Which is not to say that things can't be negotiated to some extent if one of you finds that the other's little habits intolerable).

There are some couples who spend most of the precious time they have together trying to make basic changes to each other's character, neither being able to accept the other on his own terms. But trying to turn your lover into someone else by challenging every characteristic which you perceive to be a shortcoming is a self-defeating task.

During the honeymoon period, most couples turn a blind eye to imperfections, seeing them as cute or engaging. Such is the intensity of desire during this initial period together that both partners will deliberately repress any criticism they might have of each other. There is a deep anxiety not to put any pressure on a newly-burgeoning affair and so partners are prepared to tolerate each other's shortcomings to a much greater degree than later in the relationship. The case of Mark and Harry is one example of this.

## *Making Gay Relationships Work*

Mark hates the way Harry whistles around the house. He can't explain why he finds it so irritating, the whistling just sets his teeth on edge. For the first year of their partnership, Mark was happy to tolerate the whistling, even finding it pleasant, but now all that has changed. Mark realised that Harry whistled when he was happy and in a good mood, but he still felt the need to challenge Harry every time he whistled.

**Harry**: It would be a Saturday morning, or some other time when I felt particularly relaxed. I didn't even realise I was whistling - it's just something I do when I shave. For no reason at all Mark would come knocking on the bathroom door, demanding I stop. I couldn't understand his anger.

**Mark**: It was just so tuneless.

**Harry**: Not to me it wasn't. I knew what tune I was whistling.

**Mark**: Anyway, it got on my nerves and I really couldn't stand it. You know that feeling you get when someone scratches their nail down a blackboard? It was like that. I know it sounds trivial, but now I could scream every time I hear it.

Eventually Harry began to feel victimised for what he considered a harmless activity. He confronted Mark with his annoyance and together they tried to work it out. When Harry explained that his whistling was an expression of his happiness to be at home and at leisure with his favourite person, Mark began to feel guilty about his intolerance. He apologised to Harry and said that he would try to accept the whistling and not be so cross about it in future. He would have preferred it if Harry had made an oath never to purse his lips again, but realised it was unreasonable to try and control someone to that extent. He had to accept that his partner was not as perfect as he would have liked him to be. Now when Harry whistles Mark puts on a record or vacuums the carpet.

This is a minor example, but illustrates how small irritations can be thought of as disappointing imperfections in a partner. By all means try to work it out together, but bear in mind that if you are going to try and change your partner in fundamental ways, you will introduce into his mind that you would prefer it if he were someone else. So if there is something you find imperfect in your partner ask yourself, before raising it with him, "I may not like it, but that's the way he is. Can I accept this small imperfection without it diminishing the love that I feel for him?"

Most of the "imperfections" we are talking about are inconsequential (he likes listening to music by a composer you actively loathe; he tells the same jokes every time you go out to a dinner party); most such things can be accommodated into a loving relationship, but some imperfections should not be accepted. Anything which impinges on your dignity, safety or health cannot be tolerated. You don't have to accept abuse - physical, verbal or emotional from your partner. For instance, if he constantly tries to humiliate you in front of your friends, then that is not an acceptable imperfection. If he beats you up when you disagree with him, that is totally out of order. A lover who violates your human rights is not entitled to trust, respect or acceptance.

Quiet acceptance of each other's minor faults is a sign of a truly deep committed and happily mature relationship.

## Manipulation

It is surprising how many people try to bring childish behaviour into their adult relationships. Because they could get their own way with their parents by shouting, screaming and creating general mayhem, they imagine similar antics will work with their lover. These rather unsubtle techniques are generally refined as we get older, but their origin is in no doubt. Most of us have seen the spectacle of a child screaming and crying in a shop in order to embarrass its mother into buying sweets. Later in life we might bring this same method to bear on our lover in order to get our own way. It might be a form of emotional blackmail—a veiled threat that you will not love him if he doesn't give you what you want—or other manipulative techniques that are described elsewhere in this book.

These shenanigans have no place in a mature relationship which hopes to bring love and commitment to its participants. None of the ideas contained in this book will be attainable by partners who insist on manipulating each other with the use of these childish games. You will not be able to claim that you respect, trust or accept your partner if you secretly know that you manipulate him with the deliberate use of hurtful remarks, humiliating public arguments or by creating jealousy by going off with other people to "teach him a lesson". A mature lover doesn't go in for dramatic exits during arguments or for exposing his partner to long periods of unexplained silence.

If you want your relationship to work, then you have to watch out for these techniques and stop yourself using them. In short: if this is your style, then it's time to grow up and start to enjoy being an adult.

# Chapter Five:

# Ringing the changes

When a relationship first begins, it may feel as though all your prayers have been answered. The person you've fallen in love with has all the qualities you've been seeking: he's good-looking, charming, co-operative and—best of all—extremely sexy. You can't get enough of each other and find yourselves making love at every opportunity, with no sign of boredom or exhaustion. Your libido goes haywire and your lover's every move sends you into paroxysms of lust. You spend nights on end trying all kinds of new and exotic sex games. You have romantic evenings holding hands in front of the TV, sharing secret jokes in restaurants or furtively rubbing knees in the cinema. The "symptoms" of this ecstatic beginning time are described by Dorothy Tennov in her book *Love and Limerence:*

1. thoughts of the loved person begin to intrude at all times of night and day;

2. there is an intense desire for the love object to reciprocate the feelings;

3. the feeling of walking on air when the loved one shows evidence of reciprocating;

4. a general intensifying of feelings which thrusts other concerns into the background;

5. emphasising the lover's positive attributes and ignoring the negative ones. Sexual attraction is a prime element in all this.

It seems like heaven.

This is called the honeymoon period and in most cases it lasts between six and thirty months before the intensity begins to fade. The sexual jamboree gradually diminishes and real life comes back into focus. Work commitments start to take on their former importance in your life; disagreements in the family which took a back seat now start to look serious again; debts still have to be paid; the house still has to be cleaned and, if you've moved in together, there is a whole new shared lifestyle to get used to.

Now your eyes begin to focus on the irritating little habits which you were prepared to tolerate while you were on extended honeymoon: his feet smell terribly, he snores loudly, he is untidy and is bringing mayhem to your previously ordered existence. You ask him not to leave dishes unwashed in the sink and he promises that he won't, but the amount of dirty crockery accumulates into mountainous proportions.

Why should I do all the washing up? you growl. How come it's always my job to tidy the sitting room when we have guests? Real life has returned and with it comes the first danger point.

For those who are in love with love—the intensely obsessional kind with lots of romance and sex—this might seem like the end of the relationship. They feel they've "fallen out of love" because things have cooled off. Is it time to move on and try to capture the magic with someone else? Unfortunately, those who want to be in rapturous love all their lives are bound for disappointment. However much they try to avoid the mundane in their relationship and however much they resent the calming down and diluted intensity, it always happens. However many partners we have, the honeymoon must always end sooner or later.

This is the first of what will be many changes during the lifetime of an extended relationship, and also the time when many will call it a day. Because things have become less frantic and intense, some gay men will judge their relationship to have reached its end. They worry because they no longer make love every night or because the object of their affections doesn't occupy every waking moment any more. But this is not failure; it is simply an indication that a relationship is maturing. Passionate love is changing to what has been termed companionate love. The next phase won't be so intensely thrilling but it will have new rewards and pleasures.

From now on the relationship can deepen, time will allow the partners to become companions on a much deeper level.

These changes in the nature and dynamics of a relationship have been studied and analysed in great detail by American researchers David P. McWhirter and Andrew

## Making Gay Relationships Work

Mattison ("The Male Couple - how relationships develop" - Prentice-Hall, 1984). They divided the development of gay partnerships into six stages. Briefly summarised these stages are as follows:

**Stage One:** *Blending* (approximately the first year). This is possibly the most intense phase, the one which I have called the Honeymoon Period. During this time, when sexual activity between the partners is likely to be at its peak, jealousy is more keenly felt and the interest partners show for each other verges on obsessive. The relationship and its exploration are of paramount importance and other considerations have to take a back seat. The partners are likely to be so absorbed in each other that they may become, for a while, isolated and unsociable with others. They prefer to do everything together, and submerge their individual identities, overlooking each other's faults and taking great care to avoid conflict and arguments and any other confrontation which might threaten the stability of the relationship. Sexual exclusivity is very common at this stage.

The gay writer Hugo Irwin described the feelings associated with Blending beautifully in an article he wrote for *Capital Gay*: "In '81 I met a boy who I went out with for three years. I discovered the painful thrill of parting for a weekend, the listless sense of love that filled no purpose but to serve his every desire. I knew his smell, his touch and his feel, and he taught me everything there was to know about sex and how to make 'it' happen."

**Stage Two**: which McWhirter and Mattison called *Nesting*, runs approximately from the first to the third year. In this period the partners become a little less obsessed with each other and much of their energy will be directed at making a home together. The level of sexual activity may still be high, but it is likely to be less urgent. The second stage may also see a mixture of positive and negative feelings about the relationship which lead to a sense of ambivalence about it. As the intensity of the honeymoon period lessens, doubts surface about the partner's continued interest. The changes may not be recognised for what they are—a natural progression—and be perceived as "falling out of love". This is a danger point where many relationships founder.

**Stage Three:** *Maintaining* occurs around the third to the fifth year. The partners will have changed considerably by this time, and their individual characters—which have been submerged in order to establish an identity as a couple—will once more emerge and take centre stage. There will be an increased desire for each individual to have time away from the relationship and pursue interests separately from the partner. There will also be more willingness to take risks, to speak what had previously been thought of as threatening, and to confront the issues which have been avoided. The partners will become better at dealing with conflicts as they work out their own system of coping. Traditions will be established within the relationships and anniversaries and other special occasions will become increasingly important, giving the relationship a greater feeling of substance and reality. It is also likely that those who have not formally come out to their family will find that their partnership is increasingly recognised and accepted by parents and other family members, even though it may not be specifically identified as homosexual in nature.

**Stage Four:** *Collaborating*, runs from approximately the sixth to the tenth year and some of the characteristics in this period include the feeling of security and dependability within the relationship. It might also increase the "taking for granted" element, in which partners no longer recognise the importance of the relationship and simply exist within it. Sexual activity is likely to become less frequent between the partners, with more temptation to explore sexually outside the relationship. Any 'outside' activity is likely to be seen as less threatening to the primary relationship than it would have done in previous years. The couple will be building up their shared resources and consolidating their home and material possessions. The independence that was emerging in the previous stage will, during the next stage, become established, and both partners will feel more comfortable being their own man with less need to answer to each other.

**Stage Five:** *Trusting* from the tenth to the twentieth year. The partners will feel more and more "at one" in the relationship. They will have come to accept that the likelihood is that they'll be together until one of them dies. They are likely to merge money and possessions in order to become a single unit from a material point of view. Once again, the danger of taking each other for granted is ever-present and can cause conflicts. It is at this time that men in gay relationships are likely to experience what other writers have called The Male Menopause, when the ageing process becomes most apparent and a kind of mourning for lost youth can result in a withdrawal from partner and other friends.

**Stage Six:** *Repartnering*, twenty years and more. The partnership which were studied showed the participants

110

drawing closer again during this period. They regained much of the interest they had in each other during the first stage, and began to spend more and more time together, eventually spending most of their time in each other's company. Much of the distance that had opened up between them since they first met decreased, and they became closer than at most other times in their partnership. A lot of time was spent reminiscing about their life together, and a new and comfortable affection grew between them. There was also a renewed interest in sex together.

McWhirter and Mattison analysed the lives of more than 150 gay couples before they reached their conclusions, but like everything else connected with human affairs, the study cannot give an exact picture of a 'typical' gay relationship - no such thing exists. It should also be noted that the study was completed before AIDS became a major issue in the lifestyle of gay men.

The stages the researchers identified were by no means fixed. Rather than moving in a straight line, McWhirter and Mattison suggested that the stages should be seen as running along a spring which is lying on its side - moving back and forth, up and down as well as across. Partners will be moving at different speeds, too, entering different stages at different times and moving back and forth occasionally. This can cause serious problems.

Moving from the honeymoon period to the second, cooler, era, can be especially fraught. Naturally if one partner is still wildly, passionately in love and still phoning his lover at work five times a day, he might feel that something is drastically wrong if his lover begins not to reciprocate with the same enthusiasm. This is how Jimmy and Neville experienced it.

"We'd had a wonderful year since we first met, running up to bed at every opportunity, laying there for hours wrapped in each others arms, trying every new position we could think of," said Neville. "It was a time of real giving. We shared everything about each other and I never seemed to tire of Jimmy's body. We'd leave each other silly little notes, and sit together at parties, completely wrapped up in each other and totally ignoring everyone else. It was delirious. And I mean that literally. I couldn't concentrate on my work properly for thinking about him. I neglected my friends and family. I just wanted to be with him all the time."

This was fine so long as the feelings were shared by both partners, but then Neville started to notice that Jimmy wasn't quite as keen to have sex every night; the little love notes remained unanswered and he started to stay late at the office to catch up with work. Neville says:

"I was devastated and convinced it was all over, or that he'd found someone else. The first time he said: 'Do you mind if we don't have sex tonight?' I was shattered. I felt our world had fallen apart. Then I called him one day at work and his secretary said would I mind if he called me back later as he was busy. He'd never put me second to anything before. It was like a knife in the heart. I became a real tragedy queen, imagining all kinds of things. I was convinced that we were breaking up."

This was because Jimmy was beginning to move into the second stage, while Neville was still firmly at stage one. Neither of them realised what was happening and were plagued by thoughts of the kind: "It's not like it used to be - is it all over?"

Being deeply involved in a relationship sometimes makes it difficult to stand back and see what is happening. Neville could not overcome the feelings of hurt and doom in order to see that the change in the relationship was inevitable and perfectly normal.

The honeymoon period of any relationship is often a bewildering mixture of intense happiness and sharp pain. It is an exhilarating time and one which most people enjoy. Indeed, some people get such a kick from the overblown emotions that they become reluctant to move on to the less concentrated phases. It is this search for endless romance that can cause relationships to break down. Just bear in mind that although the honeymoon is great, what follows can be more wonderful yet.

The danger in undergoing this change is that partners will forget that continuous effort and assessment is required to keep things going. Just because you're beginning to settle down together doesn't mean that you can forget to let your partner know that you will love him. The occasional overt statement of love can sometimes greatly reassure a partner and clear up any lingering doubts that the relationship is still strong. Partners may be close, but they aren't mind-readers and although it doesn't mean you have to utter those immortal worlds "I Love You" every five minutes (and many men have profound difficulty saying those words at all) there are other little signs you can give to indicate that you still feel good about being together. A little unexpected knee rub, perhaps, a kiss or an affectionate hug can all

113

reinforce your commitment. A beautifully cooked meal of the loved one's favourite dish, presented with the aim to please can be reassuring - as can a thousand and one other little gestures which indicate that the partners still consider each other special. Don't neglect or devalue such signals - they are important.

Accepting the gradual change in the nature of a relationship is the first and key way to make it succeed. If you are startled to realise that your feelings have changed, step back and ask: "What is different?" You should come up with one of three answers: "I've changed", "My partner's changed" or "The nature of our relationship has changed." But change is growth, not death. Only inanimate objects don't mature; a living organism (which is what a relationship is) will constantly shift aspect and emphasis. Acknowledge these changes, measure them and accommodate them.

Sometimes the change is brought about by the personal growth of one of the partners. As they go through life their experiences will shape the way they develop. An optimist can be embittered, for instance, by a succession of disappointments; a shy person can grow in confidence; a criminal can reform; a saint can fall from grace. If we look back at ourselves as we were ten or fifteen years ago, we will see someone who was substantially different to the person we are today. The change might have been gradual, but it will have been emphatic. The fact that you are in a relationship does not mean that other things will have stopped happening in your life. Your career might take off, you might find you have a calling to some great task or you might simply get itchy feet and want to travel.

We'll look more closely at coping with this kind of change in a separate chapter.

## Leaving The Single Life Behind

For someone who is coming to a relationship after an extended period of being a single, free agent, there can be problems making the adjustment to being part of a couple.

Naturally there is no reason why a relationship should become a prison in which all liberty is forfeit and all independence sacrificed. Both of you can—and must—retain your own identities while enjoying the fruits of partnership. In order to manage this, you need to make a sensible, planned approach and be prepared to compromise a little. To enjoy the benefits of a loving partnership you have to accept an element of restriction. One of your new responsibilities is consultation with your partner about decisions which are going to affect both your lives. Choices which would, in your former single life, have been made without reference to anyone else, now need to be discussed. Suppose, for instance, your boss offers you a chance of a lifetime, he wants you to spend a year working in the branch office in Tahiti. You've always longed to visit Tahiti, you want the experience of living in a different culture. This is a golden opportunity to realise your ambition.

Previously you would have said "yes, yes, yes" and signed the contract without further ado, but now you have commitments at home. Your partner has a job, too, and while you may think this is the chance of a lifetime, he might be horrified at the idea of (a) your being separated for a whole year or (b) having to give up his own job to go with you.

Less dramatic circumstances can also cause conflict, of course. If your partner always gets home from work before

115

you do and prepares the evening meal, then you would have to think twice about accepting an invitation for an after-work drink with one of your colleagues which would make you late. It would be thoughtless and impolite not to let your partner know that you won't be home at your usual time and that you won't need the meal.

If making such consultations irritates you, then it's clear you haven't really let go of your single status. If you get angry because your partner seems to get in the way of your plans, then you need to do some serious thinking. It may be that there was more reward for you in your single state than there is in a partnership. Now is the time to take stock and make out the emotional balance sheet; weigh up the debits and credits of your relationship. If, in the end, you think that the disadvantages of being in a partnership outweigh the advantages, then a complete reappraisal of your relationship and your attitudes towards it are needed.

It is usual to experience a kind of mourning for the life you've given up. You're bound to miss some of the old routines and the former circumstances. Hopefully you were prepared to make the sacrifice because you thought that what your partner would provide was more fulfilling than what you had before. And, indeed, if you both work on it, your partnership can give you everything you had hoped it would.

## Letting Go of Old Loves

Often the difficulties we encounter in the early days of a relationship are really unresolved problems from previous relationships. We all know about the "rebound effect", when a partner shattered by one broken affair will rush into another in the hope that it will relieve the pain of parting.

Often this is not a conscious decision or a deliberate policy, but it happens nevertheless. This does not mean that because a new relationship has been started with the (maybe unconscious) desire to replace a lost one, that it has no value. Indeed, it can rapidly take on a life of its own if you are both determined that it will work. If the conflicts brought in from the previous relationship can be resolved without too much acrimony, you can build from there.

If a relationship which was highly prized has ended, then there will be a number of unavoidable consequences - intense pain and depression are the most obvious. Then will come the loss of confidence. The breakdown of what was considered a primary relationship can have devastating effects of self-esteem. Those who've split up may be plagued with doubts about their value as a person, about their loveability and their attractiveness. Next may come a period of grief with all its attendant confusion. With patience these problems can be resolved; time will help you let go of your broken relationship and recover to love again.

However, if you try to circumvent the undoubted unpleasantness of this recovery period by starting another relationship too soon, you will simply carry the problems into your new partnership. Often your new lover will be aware of your pain, and if he is wise he will make allowances for it. But if he is unaware of what is going on, then he may feel that the conflicts are somehow his fault.

## Married Gay Men

Not all previous relationships will necessarily have been homosexual in nature; many gay men enter into heterosexual marriage. There can be a lot of different—and perfectly valid—reasons for doing this, and some married

117

gay men are extremely positive about their marriages. But many are not and are relieved to be free to pursue the life they truly desire. If you have left a marriage or heterosexual relationship in order to fulfil your true nature there may be added complications in making the transition to gay life. If, for instance, there are children, it will be much harder for you to make a clean break and they are likely to be a constant reminder of your previous life. But whether your previous relationship was homosexual or heterosexual, the same "letting-go" period will be required. It may even take longer for those leaving a marriage though, because not only are you letting go of a partner, you are letting go of a particular way of life. The problems which can be connected with changing from a heterosexual to a homosexual lifestyle include:

- Shock and bewildered reactions from family and friends - perhaps even more intense than for unmarried gays who come out.

- Leaving children behind. Gay fathers are unlikely to be awarded custody of their off-spring, although it has been known.

- Bringing expectations of a heterosexual way of life to a gay relationships. The same rules don't always apply.

- There is a likelihood that you will be taking up a gay lifestyle relatively late in life. Problems of adjustment might be increased by this factor.

- Your new freedoms might cause you to over-react. It is common for gay men to begin their real lives much later than heterosexuals - we have to spend much more of our youth sorting out our attitudes to our sexuality, perhaps trying to overcome negative feelings about it. It is not uncommon to see gay men experiencing what amounts to a delayed adolescence once they have wholeheartedly thrown themselves into their new and liberating way of life.

One of the marvellous things for gay men who "find themselves" after a period of heterosexual marriage is the sense of relief they experience on freeing themselves from the ties. It does not necessarily indicate that they didn't love their wife or enjoy the marriage, it's just that the homosexual desire which they've longed to express will have more meaning for them. Often, when the dust settles and feelings have been resolved, a new and friendly relationship emerges between husband, wife and new lover. I have met several gay couples who have extremely close and caring friendships with their previous wives and their children. People are surprisingly adaptable when it comes to adjusting to new situations.

Men coming into gay relationships from a heterosexual marriage often make a great success of their new life. If a couple are determined and if their commitment to each other is strong enough, they can overcome all the problems, but it won't happen overnight. Patience is the keyword.

## Isolation

During the honeymoon period, when lovers naturally spend a great deal of time together, they may become almost reclusive, revelling in their new-found love and excluding or neglecting old friends. This is understandable, and almost everyone does it for a while. But in the end your relationship will not be able to satisfy every emotional and social need you have. If you want to spend the majority of your leisure time together, fine, but it is wise for you retain your circle of friends and continue to find new ones. If you look to your lover for all your social contact, you may eventually find you have become unhealthily dependent on him.

Having other friends, other social outlets (whether alone or together) means you don't lose sight of yourself as an individual. That part of your life which is separate from your relationship (and work is normally the biggest portion of that) can keep you growing and giving you the stimulation your partner can't. If, for instance, you like amateur dramatics, but your partner doesn't, don't give it up. Pursuing your hobby might mean that you have to spend time away from your beloved, but it will ensure that you keep sight of who you are, and why you are unique. Being always referred to as "Bob and Carl" or "Dave and Mike" by your friends might seem cosy and reassuring, but it's not good if you're *never* seen as a person in your own right.

If you have friends with whom your partner doesn't get on, don't be too quick to give them up - see them when he isn't around. Many partners—particularly after the first two or three years of a relationship—nominate one or more evenings in the week when they'll go off and see their own friends or do their own thing. But please negotiate this, don't impose it unilaterally - and ensure you both understand what the limits of "doing your own thing" are). Not only will this introduce some variety into both your social lives, it will give you something to compare notes about. Having other friends brings an aspect to the relationship which shouldn't be undervalued.

Sharing each other's existing circle of friends is another good idea. So long as both partners are happy with the arrangement, leading an individual social life as well as a joint one can bolster the relationship rather than diminish it.

## Money Matters

Sex and money will probably be the two most contentious areas of your life together. Sex is discussed elsewhere, but what about your financial life? How are you going to work an arrangement that suits both of you, and is fair? For heterosexuals there is almost always a large imbalance between the husband and wife's income. Two men living together are more likely to match each other financially. But what if one gay partner has a much more substantial salary than the other? What if one is unemployed or a student? How much of your money will you pool and how much will you keep for yourselves?

There are several ways of working out how you'll share living expenses, depending on your circumstances. Naturally if you both have good salaries which will easily cover your expenses and still leave reasonable amounts of disposable income, you can simply split expenses down the middle. But if there is a large disparity of income, where one partner is earning substantially more than the other, different arrangements might be considered. One is for each partner to put everything they earn into a common pool and then withdraw whatever each needs for expenses. This is the simplest method and it can work for some people. It isn't without pitfalls, though, one of which is that the person earning the higher wage might begin to feel exploited if he is pooling all of his resources and the other is generously drawing from it to buy what appear to be luxury items. Another possible consequence is that one partner might feel guilty about spending the other's money.

Another option is for each partner to contribute an agreed proportion towards joint financial obligations according to his means. If your salary is half that of your partner then you could contribute a third of the expenses and your partner two thirds. Contributions from the higher wage earner could be increased if the lifestyle that you have, or special treats, are beyond the means of the lower paid partner. What each of you has left after paying the agreed proportion would be your own discretionary money to spend as you like. It seems that for most couples this is the favoured method. It works well so long as both partners are happy with the ratio and neither contributor feels exploited. There need be no guilt about buying items which the other partner didn't approve of, so long as you're using your own discretionary money to do it.

The purchase of expensive or large-scale items which will be of mutual benefit is a matter of negotiation. If you want to buy a car, for instance, then you will need to think very carefully about the issues connected with it. Who will use it most? What ongoing expenses will there be, like maintenance and rising fuel costs? How will you decide which model will be right for you? The same goes for such items as microwave ovens, washing machines, stereo equipment, video recorders and so on. If these are to be joint purchases, you must work out beforehand whether you can afford them and who will pay what toward their purchase. When you are purchasing expensive items together it is important that you make some sort of contract beforehand about how they will be disposed of in the event of your relationship ending. A little thought at the beginning can save a lot of heartache at the end.

Negotiation is the answer to all these issues. Read more about relationship skills in Chapter Seven.

## The Macho Trap

Men are tough, active and go-getters; women are gentle, nurturing and sensitive. Women talk about their lives and their feelings; men talk about football. These are the common images of what men and women are supposed to be. We've been taught to accept them all our lives, and most of us have thoroughly internalised them. And although efforts are being made to change them, the ideas are still very strong and permeate all parts of Western culture.

On the face of it, although men hold the power in society, it is women who are generally happier and better adjusted emotionally. This is probably because women have been encouraged from an early age to pay attention to their, and other peoples', feelings. They spend a lot of time talking to each other about their reactions to life events. If women are upset, they are more likely to cry and share their misery with their best friend. Men, on the other hand—unless they've trained themselves well—are likely to take the hard knocks in life with a stiff upper lip, keeping their true feelings well out of sight.

The results can be disastrous for individual men, who have kept traumatic feelings locked inside themselves for fear that other will see them as weak or unmanly. Big boys don't cry—more's the pity.

When two men get together in an intimate relationship it is possible that one or both may not find it easy to "open up" about intimate feelings. Or if one partner is able to discuss emotional issues, the other may freeze up and withdraw from the conversation. Many of us are victims of

123

our conditioning, our role as men is pre-ordained for us and most of us are obliged to play it to some extent.

Researchers into homosexual relationships have shown that lesbians are far more skilled than gay men at tackling the emotional problems that arise within their partnerships. Lesbians, like all women, have been conditioned to feel OK in exposing their inner vulnerabilities, whereas gay men really have to work hard at letting down the defences they have erected to protect their sense of maleness.

Eric found this a particular problem with his partner Geoff:

**Eric**: When we first started out we didn't seem to have any problems talking to each other, we talked about everything. And when we made love we gave up our bodies completely to each other. That seemed like a wonderful way of communicating our feelings - the closeness said it all. But after a while I realised that there are some things you can't say with your body, you have to articulate them. I wanted to know how Geoff was feeling about the relationship. I'd sensed him drawing away from me over a period of months, but I couldn't work out what was wrong. The more I asked him to talk about it, the less communicative he became. I just had to try and guess the problem. As you can imagine, my imagination was working overtime. When I said things like 'Is something wrong? Have I done something to upset you?' He would just say 'No' and change the subject. I was very worried, and eventually came to the conclusion that we were on a slippery slope and that the relationship would soon end. Eventually, from one of his colleagues, I discovered that Geoff was having horrendous problems at work, which he hadn't told me about. He was trying to cope with it alone because he was concerned that if I thought he was making a mess of his job he would be regarded as a total failure. Like so many men, his identity was totally wrapped up in his career. I tried to talk to him about it, but there was no way that he was going to open up. He said he could sort things out in his own way. I felt excluded and resented it. The issue was clouding our whole life, but I simply couldn't get him to discuss it. He became almost reclusive and finally I had to leave him because I couldn't stand seeing him being burned up by his refusal to let me— or anybody else—help. It may seem a terrible thing to walk out on someone who is in such a state, but I couldn't bear it."

Most of the suggestions in this book will depend for their success on effective communication, the ability of partners to talk to each other on a level that they may be unused to, and which they may find threatening. However, if a relationship is going to thrive, it needs partners to acknowledge the absolute importance of opening up and sharing feelings. It may be uncomfortable, it may be painful, but it has to be done.

If you find it particularly difficult to let down your defences it might be worthwhile joining some kind of group therapy session which would help you, in a safe environment, to experiment with the notion of vulnerability. The experience of laying your innermost perceptions of yourself on the line to a group of strangers is a powerful one. It can help liberate you from the fear of sharing your terrors, your sadness and your humanity with other human beings. Beware, though, of groups organised by extreme religious organisations, they are likely to make you feel worse about yourself rather than better.

## Be Your Own Therapist

If such a group is impossible for you, then there are simple exercises you and your partner can do together. Mostly they involve a conscious effort to look inwards and reflect, something which many men have assiduously avoided.

Some people find the following an effective way of building trust and practising communication skills:

Switch off the TV, the radio, unplug the phone and dispense with distractions. Then spend some time with your partner, in a relaxed and secure environment (perhaps over a leisurely meal at home) talking about your childhood, the way you grew up and what you felt about your parents. During this search of memory and emotion, you should each be prepared to accept and allow the other his feelings. It is important not to try and interpret each other's reactions or to dictate how people *should* feel in a given circumstance; just acknowledge what your partner says without approving or disapproving of it; merely acknowledge that it is real at that moment.

If you try this casting-your-mind-back exercise together, don't turn it into a simple story-telling session - that's just a strategy for avoiding feelings. We are not just telling jolly anecdotes about our childhood, we are trying to explore feelings that we may never have confronted before.

The kind of issues which you should each strive to talk about at length and in detail are: how do you really feel about your parents? (Never mind the line you always give people when you're talking about your family, this is the moment of truth.) Love and hate are the issues and they shouldn't be avoided. If your parents are dead, imagine yourself talking to them as if they were still alive - is there anything that you left unsaid? Is there anything that life has taught you that you wish you'd known before they died? How did you get on with your father? Did you feel that he was distant or close? Were you afraid of him? Do you feel he owes you an apology for anything that happened early in your life - or vice versa? What about your mother? What did you truly feel about her?

If you've never uttered fundamental criticism of your parents before, or if you never even knew that this was the way you felt about them, then it may come as a shock when you say it for the first time. You may feel guilty, disloyal or even wicked for pinpointing your parents' weaknesses or injustices. Or you may feel relieved that you've actually admitted it at last. Whatever your feeling - intense love, vague resentment, regret, outright hatred or all these things, say it. Put it into words and acknowledge it.

Your partner should listen patiently, and maybe question you about what you are saying, but he should be careful to offer no judgement or interpretation or explanation. You are there to help each other and to build trust. You must both feel secure that neither will ever repeat to anyone else what has been said between you.

If you get into the habit of sharing such feelings, and you feel safe to do so, your relationship will be enhanced immeasurably. You will have accepted your vulnerability, and that will be of enormous value when problems arise later in your life together. Instead of keeping silent, you will be able to confront your dilemmas and that will make them much easier to solve and much less threatening to the stability of your union.

127

# Chapter Six:

# Other people's approval

One of history's best known homosexuals was the composer Tchaikovsky. Because of the time in which he lived he was obliged to suppress and deny his sexuality. In Tsarist Russia (as in just about every other society of that period) it was expected that men and women would marry and lead conventional heterosexual lives. Even as an artist, Tchaikovsky was not allowed—or perhaps did not allow himself—to defy the strictly observed customs of the time. Although he led a secret homosexual life, he also bowed to pressure and married. It was a disaster for all concerned, and led him to write in a letter to his gay brother, Modest: "All that is left is to pretend. But to pretend to the end of one's life is the highest torment."

If you are not open about your sexuality with all your close family, and your colleagues, it follows that your relationship, too, will be a closed book to them. Trying to sustain a relationship in constant secrecy is difficult if not impossible but, nevertheless, many gay couples try it. Posing as flatmates in order to live together without disapproval is a favourite ploy. However successfully you think you have concealed your affair, people are more worldly these days, and many would guess the truth; it doesn't take neighbours long to observe your lifestyle and put two and two together. The only way you could possibly hide the truth from those in the neighbourhood would be to make up elaborate lies about your being "brothers living together for convenience" or for your to import occasional girlfriends in order to allay suspicions. Meanwhile elaborate smoke screens have to be erected every time family or friends visit - two bedrooms so that no one will get the idea that you sleep together, no overt signs of a gay lifestyle, constant distance and denial.

This happened to Julian and Eric who live in London and who tried to convince their parents that they were simply sharing accommodation and not a life together.

**Julian**: Whenever Eric's parents came over to visit I would have to move all my things out of our shared bedroom and into the spare room, pretending that was where I slept. We had to gather up all gay newspapers and remove anything from the room that might have given the game away. When his parents were in the house they would expect me to make myself scarce so that they could have time with him alone. I was treated like a lodger who was there for financial convenience rather than someone who was important in Eric's life. I don't know whether it was because they suspected the truth or what, but they were quite hostile to me. I felt terrible. Not only that but Eric had to go along with this sham. He had to deny me, too, by saying nothing when his parents were giving me the cold shoulder.

## Making Gay Relationships Work

**Eric**:  At the time I felt it as the right thing to do. I had no intention of coming out to my parents. It was too painful to contemplate. And even though I loved Julian, I couldn't introduce him as my lover - they'd have hit the roof. So we kept up the pretence. I didn't feel too bad about it, it just didn't seem like there was an alternative. However, I was always very relieved when they went home because the we could relax again. I was always a little bit nervous that one day they'd call on us unexpectedly and catch us at it or something.

**Julian**: I had come out to my parents a long time ago and I couldn't understand Eric's reluctance. I would encourage him to tell them, but he wouldn't even consider the idea. So when my parents came to visit, he insisted that we go through the same malarkey in case his parents and my parents ever met. I felt like an idiot, and I felt cheated that I couldn't share this important thing in my life with my mother and father.

The situation which Julian and Eric created is fairly common. An excellent and very funny  illustration of where all this deceit can lead is the theme of a film called "The Wedding Banquet". The male lovers in the movie try to keep the truth of their relationship from visiting parents - with catastrophic consequences. If you haven't seen it, try to get a copy from your local video shop and ask yourselves whether the mistakes made by the characters in the story are familiar.

This denial of your relationship has two major effects: it robs it of dignity and then denies it space to grow. It can do nothing but reinforce the idea in the minds of both partners that their love is in some way disgraceful and undesirable, something to be hidden. The relationship is almost certainly doomed unless this idea can be unloaded. How is a relationship to gain strength when its mere existence is a cause of shame for the participants? Instead of being a source of happiness, your partnership is a constant stress.

The inability to develop the relationship will also have dire consequences upon it; without validation and support from other people, it is likely to falter. We need friends with whom we can compare notes, show off our partner and simply socialise together. The acknowledgement by our peers (and ideally our family) that they accept our loving relationship validates it and gives it enormous strength. This may seem like a contradiction of other advice given—that you don't need other people's approval—but in fact you do need some sort of support network in which to function. No individual or relationship can survive in a vacuum.

The kind of support you need is that which is freely given by those who love you, not that which has to be begged for and which involves a denial of the truth. We need to feel that we are part of human society, and there are plenty of people out there who will be friendly towards our relationship if we'll permit them to be. You don't need approval from the whole world, only from that part which is important to you.

Some partners in secretive relationships will open the closet door to other gay friends, while keeping it firmly closed to the rest of the world. This is better than nothing, of course. Gay friends will, in the main, accept the relationship and give it some reality. They will, unless they are malicious and jealous, wish it well. But when gay socialising is over, and the rest of the world has to be faced, the closet door will be closed and the heat will be turned up once more. There is no need to feel that you have to "shout it from the roof tops"—most people will be uninterested in your domestic arrangements anyway—but you should make those people who are important to you, and who can influence your feelings, party to your lifestyle.

The sheer relief of being "out" with parents, family and friends is wonderful, and it is heartening to discover how accepting they can be. Initial fears about revealing the truth often dissolve completely when loving acceptance is experienced. I have written about coming out generally in my book "How to be a Happy Homosexual" (GMP Publishers), and I am utterly convinced that being honest with our nearest and dearest is the only way to make a successful gay life and a fulfilling relationship.

In the case of Eric and Julian, the pressure eventually proved too much. Julian became increasingly frustrated at the humiliation he suffered in front of Eric's parents, and reluctantly came to the conclusion that he did not want to continue living this underground existence.

**Julian**: I felt depressed by the whole charade. My dignity was compromised and I began to get very angry with Eric. I had to tell him that I didn't want to live this way. It was terrible to think of splitting up, but I didn't see where the relationship could go. We had a tearful confrontation and I told him I would have to move out. He begged me to stay and promised that he would try to come out to his parents.

**Eric**: I don't know which prospect I found most daunting - coming out to Mum and Dad or losing Julian. I thought about it for a long time and, after a lot of sleepless nights, I came to the conclusion that if Julian moved out and I kept up the pretence with my parents, I would eventually be a lonely old man. After all, my parents had already had their life; their marriage was happy and they didn't need me. I needed a life of my own that made some kind of sense to me. So I did it. I went round to their place one day and came out. It was the hardest day of my life, and a dreadful trauma for them, too. They went mad, asking if I had Aids and then blaming Julian for corrupting me. I tried to explain but in the end I just had to come back home, leaving them both in tears and promising not to see them again if that's what they wanted. I was so upset I just can't tell you. It was three weeks before they contacted me, three weeks of pure hell, but they made overtures and I went round for tea. It was difficult and embarrassing and they were still trying to talk me out of it. I had to stick to my guns and come home again. Next time I went over they didn't talk about it at all, and each subsequent time I went to visit, the atmosphere was a bit easier. They stopped crying, stopped looking at me as though I was from Mars, and we resumed our relationship as before.

**Julian**: Except that they didn't talk about me, and they didn't come round to the flat.

**Eric**: That was the next hurdle. It was like having to come out to them all over again, telling them about Julian. All the wounds were re-opened, but this time they healed a bit quicker. After a year I felt confident enough to invite them round here for tea. They came and they met Julian in his new guise as my lover. It was all very fraught, but at least they did it.

**Julian**: I think they were very brave, and they really are doing their best. I know it isn't easy for them, but it isn't easy for us either. I think we'll make it in the end. We're most of the way there already. I think they're gradually accepting the idea that we aren't so bad as a couple after all. I feel much better about our relationship. I feel it has a lot more integrity now that we don't have to deny each other.

After he'd taken the plunge with his parents, Eric found that telling his friends at work was a doddle. He even found that Julian was invited on work outings and accepted as a partner.

Many homosexual couples who have taken the plunge and come out to all their friends have found that they are accepted on their own terms by most of them. Recently in a newspaper column which advised readers on modern manners, a heterosexual enquirer asked: "I wish to invite a gay friend over for dinner, but am not sure whether I should also invite his friend." This indicates that in some circles (admittedly this was a middle-class newspaper), it is acceptable to invite gay couples to straight dinner parties and other social events on their own terms. In my own case, Keith and I have had wide acceptance as a couple among our work colleagues, family and friends. We are invited to their homes and they come to ours; there is little indication that people feel uncomfortable with our lifestyle. They soon come to realise that it doesn't differ much from their own for these purposes. Naturally, if they did feel uncomfortable in our home or were critical of the way we live, they would not be invited again and it is unlikely that the friendship would continue.

How you are accepted as a couple will very much depend on the circles in which you move. There is little doubt that you will receive some rejection, but that shouldn't put you off. People who can't accept your relationship are not people that have any business being in your life anyway. Besides which, homophobes are invariably miserable bores.

By all means try to change people's attitudes with reason if their friendship is important to you, but don't compromise your living arrangements in order not to make them feel uncomfortable. For instance, if they come to a party at your home and you've also invited gay friends, they should accept on those terms. If it disturbs them to be in gay company, then that's their problem, not yours. There is a limit to the distance you can go in accommodating their prejudice.

### "Mum, Dad - This is My Lover"

When you introduce your lover to the family, you might be surprised to find how quickly they take to him, often welcoming this honorary member with enthusiasm. I know many gay couples who feel a warmth and acceptance from both families that has enriched them all. Take the case of Paul and Gavin, who live in a large industrial town in the north of England. Paul came out to his family when he was in his teens and Gavin did the same with his family when he was twenty-four. The reactions were mixed. For Paul, the family was totally accepting and supportive. In Gavin's case, however, his brother rejected him completely while his parents resisted the news for many years until they grudgingly accepted it.

Now they have been living together for ten years, their relationship has been almost totally accepted by both families (the exception being Gavin's brother who remains distant and hostile). In many ways their love is a model of stability. Paul's sister has been married and divorced twice during the ten years they have been together.

Of course, it might not be all sweetness and light; the difficulties that arise between lovers and 'in-laws' are not always to do with homosexuality, but with the everyday conflicts of human interaction. Paul finds Gavin's mother hard going because she is demanding and thoughtless, but he continues to visit her for Gavin's sake. When Gavin's father died, both of them were expected at the funeral, and both of them attended on the same basis as Gavin's brother and sister who came with their spouses. Paul and Gavin's experience is not unique. Most gay couples who conduct themselves with dignity and who persist, find their families come to accept and respect them. It may take time, but it's worth the initial hassle and heartache.

If, however, families refuse to accept a relationship and break off contact, it may put pressure on the partnership and a resentful feeling might emerge that "This relationship has robbed me of the love of my family." Such defective reasoning should be resisted: the truth is that your family is trying to rob you of the kind of love and companionship they take for granted in their own lives. It is not the relationship which has caused you to break with your family, it is *their attitude* to it. You cannot change yourself into a heterosexual in order to relieve them of their disapproval, it is up to them to dump their objections and accept the situation as it is.

So how much effort should be put into trying to build bridges between gay couples and parents who are unwilling to accept them? This will obviously be for each individual couple to judge. Family ties have differing degrees of importance to different people. Don't give up too quickly. You may be offended or deeply hurt by your parents' reaction, and you might be disappointed at their rejection of your lover, but hopefully you'll make some effort to see it from their point of view. Parents who discover that their child is gay often suffer an enormous shock. They are ignorant of the facts, afraid for your future and anxious about the possible reactions of others. Feelings of shame, guilt and anger overwhelm them.

Their first reaction might be to thrust you away, furious that you have brought such pain to them. Many such parents have described the feeling as being like a bereavement: the familiar child has died and been replaced by an unfamiliar person who feels like a stranger. But over a period their feelings are resolved, and their love for their son resumes as before.

All this takes time, often years. During that period you have to get on with your own life. By all means make attempts to patch up misunderstanding between you, but don't compromise yourself or your partnership in order to restore relations with your family. The pain that you all feel will, in the end, be a creative force. It will release you from the burden of deceit, and it will allow your parents to accept you as a complete human being.

Many gay couples never tell their parents in so many words that their relationship is of a homosexual nature, they just allow the family to observe them together as "inseparable friends" or "close flatmates" and eventually parents get the message and begin treating them accordingly.

Some gay people have reported that the quality of their relationship with their parents has improved after they have come out. As one man described it thus:

"It was as if I'd been released from the duty of being a child. Until my parents knew the truth, I wasn't allowed to grow up. Now I have a completely different relationship with them. They talk to me like an adult and we discuss issues we never could before."

Another advantage of being out and on good terms with your parents is that if things go wrong you will have their support rather than their hostility. Andrew, a man of thirty-two from Bristol, describes his own experience.

"My boyfriend Kevin became very ill a few years ago and needed to be admitted to hospital. Naturally I was very worried about him and phoned the hospital constantly for information about his condition. I visited him every night after work and at weekends. I managed to time my visits so they didn't coincide with his family, whom we didn't get on with. Gradually his condition deteriorated and he was transferred to the intensive care unit. That was when it started to get difficult. When I rang the hospital they would only give me the most rudimentary information: 'As well as can be expected' and that sort of thing. They told me that as I wasn't a member of the immediate family they couldn't give me any further details and I should contact Kev's mother. I was furious, but there was little I could do, as Kevin had nominated his mother as next of kin, simply because he didn't realise he could nominate me. Neither of us had realised that it would become this serious so quickly. We had never been on very good terms with his family—especially not his mother—who didn't really approve of our living together. I think they had the impression that I had somehow tempted Kevin into being gay, and it was all my fault. Anyway, when I found that only immediate family were allowed to visit intensive care, I had no alternative but to ring Kev's mother and ask if she would arrange for me to see him. I was surprised when she said 'yes' and we arranged to meet at the hospital. She gave permission to the nurses for me to visit Kevin, who was on a life support system. We both went in together, all dressed up in protective clothes, and saw him lying on the bed with these pipes coming out of him and wires attached all over his body. When I saw him like that I just burst into tears. Kev's mother put her arm round my shoulder and we sat together just looking at him because he was unconscious at the time. I think when she realised how important Kev was to me, and that there was more to our relationship than just sex, she let up on the disapproval. That was the start of our getting to know each other. Kev recovered on that occasion, but it was the beginning of a long terminal illness. I'm pleased to say that by the time he died we had established a totally different and much better relationship with his family. When the end came, I really needed them, and they came through for me. I am just terribly sorry that Kev and I couldn't have had a proper relationship with them when he was well."

Although most people won't have to experience such tragic circumstances in order to bring them together, it shows that practical as well as emotional needs are served by being on good terms with each other's families.

## They Know But We Don't Talk About It

A lot of gay men simply move in with their lover and then assume that their parents will 'get the picture' without a full explanation and a painful coming out scene. In most cases this will happen, and although they might not be happy about it, most parents in that situation keep their peace and carry on as though nothing unusual is happening. Eventually, as they get to know and like the lover, they will accept and integrate him into family events. They will come to accept the relationship without ever acknowledging its real character. The researchers McWhirter and Mattison found that this stage of tacit acceptance by the family was unlikely to be reached until the relationship had been in existence for at least three years.

After a whirlwind courtship, Paul and Timothy had the feeling that they were right for each other and bought a house together. Both were close to their family but neither had come out to them as gay. They hadn't explained either that the joint house purchase was for the purpose of sustaining a romantic attachment.

The parents and brothers and sisters were disturbed by this development, but none of them asked any direct questions of the couple about the nature of their relationship. It was possible that they had discussed it among themselves in private, but they never named it in the presence of Paul or Timothy. The two men have been together for five years now and Paul tells of a significant event which says something about his parents' acceptance of Timothy and himself as a couple.

> "At Christmas each year my mother would send me a card saying 'to my dearest son'. This year she sent on which said 'From our house to your house' which, as far as I'm concerned, is her way of giving tacit approval to our relationship."

Christmas, for gay couples, can be a particularly difficult time, as the demands of an uncomprehending family conflict with the needs of their gay children. This was illustrated vividly in an article by John Lyttle, which appeared in The Independent newspaper. Mr Lyttle has given me permission to reproduce the piece here, and I am sure it will ring depressingly familiar bells with many gay couples.

> "'And you must be Richard,' my father says to my significant other. Planted in the doorway, Dad proffers a sweaty palm and flashes the fixed smile of the chat show host. How strange to witness my father trying to act *normal*. That used to be my job.
>
> I don't know why I say what I'm about to say, but I say it. I say: 'He prefers Dick.'
>
> Freudian or what? Your gay son brings his partner home for Christmas Day and the first thing out of his mouth is...
>
> The moment pauses and replays endlessly. Then, in a classic example of group telepathy, we mutually decide that I never said anything, not one single word about Richard preferring you-know-what.

141

It was many years ago and I've forgotten why I invited my then lover to Christmas over lunch with my family.

Oh, that's *such* a lie. I know *exactly* why. I did it because the parents of gay children too often expect their homosexual progeny to return automatically to the nest for the Yuletide season, an obligation seldom visited upon their heterosexual siblings.

Yes, yes, my bothers and sisters try and make surprise guest appearances. If they should fail to show, well, that's OK. They have *real* lives. Responsibilities: babies, neighbours and friends popping in, turkey to stuff, frosty in-laws to thaw. The unspoken assumption about the gay child is that you have nothing better to do, that you have a marginal existence, that otherwise you'll be...lonely this Christmas.

So you have a partner? So what? It's not like having a husband or wife, someone you'd mind being separated from. No point in inviting him; after all, he'll be going to his folks, too, won't he?

Actually, Mother Dearest, he won't. I thought Richard might come to see us.

I know it's a farce, but I have to do it, have to bring my life to the people who gave it to me, instead of leaving it behind.

My mother's voice, crackling over the line, was high and hectic, as if she were about to clap her hands and announce that she does believe in fairies (aptly enough). Bring Richard. Everyone would like to meet him.

The front room: my younger brother instantly begins to tell queer jokes: 'hear about the gay cowboys who rode into town and shot up the sheriff?' Nerves, though he'll later maintain he was putting Richard at his ease, while I wonder about such classic psychological terms as 'unconscious hostility'. A subject I'm forced to ponder through this long, long day as my mother dumps steaming Brussels sprouts into Richard's lap and my father jettisons beer down the front of his new silk shirt. Take that, and that...

My sister flirts with Richard. 'You're barking up the wrong tree,' I interrupt, as his confusion becomes comically evident. 'He's cute,' Sis hisses conspiratorially. Lunch. Everyone's on auto-pilot. The nearest and dearest are digesting, along with the turkey, the idea that my gayness isn't a solo deal—that it requires the active, not to say enthusiastic, involvement of someone else. The evidence is before them, asking for more roast potatoes and complimenting my mother's cooking. (My father stares at Richard as though he has lost his mind along with his taste buds: an honest response at last.) The knowledge is resented, but it's the best Christmas present I'll ever give them. They just don't know it yet.

You can smell the relief when Richard announces his departure. Duty has been reluctantly done: season of goodwill to all men etc. Still, I'm touched when Mum suggests I should walk Richard to the door alone. He walks down the garden path, his shirt and trousers ruined, and I have a sudden pang of guilt. He stops at the gate and looks back.

143

> The clan are clustered at the window—damned if
> they're not waving. Richard waves back. 'Next
> year,' he says, 'how about us visiting my lot?'"

A large scale investigation into the lives of gay men in Britain is being undertaken by Project Sigma (Socio-sexual Investigations into Gay Men and Aids). Preliminary findings have revealed that of 930 men they interviewed 21.8 per cent were "out" to all their family, friends and significant others in their lives; 45.1 per cent were out to most of them; 15.9 per cent were out to "a few"; 15.8 per cent were out to "less than half" and only 3.8 per cent were completely in the closet. The survey didn't tell us how successful they were in their disclosure and what kind of reactions they got, but it does indicate that fewer and fewer gay people are prepared to tolerate a completely closeted existence.

There are some straight people, of course, who can't and won't come to terms with our existence, and there are even those who devote their lives to making life more difficult for us (usually from religious conviction). Such people pale into insignificance beside those who love us and accept us. Your own dignity and strength will stand you in good stead if you are having problems with people outside, and the mutual support you can generate within the relationship will help keep you on course during these sticky patches.

# Chapter Seven:

# **Relationship skills**

Children whose parents have a combative relationship might come to believe, as they observe the interminable fights between mum and dad, that acrimony or even violence are the ways to resolve disagreements in a partnership. It's unlikely that anyone will tell them directly that there might be better ways to sort things out.

However, simply because our parents might have based their negotiations on loud, bitter, no-holds-barred fights, doesn't mean that we are doomed to take the same unyielding stance in our own relationships. If we want to approach things differently, we can.

If you were raised in a home filled with rancour and argument, then now is the time to discover new, less hurtful and more effective ways to resolve conflicts. Research into gay relationships indicates that homosexual men are much less likely than their heterosexual counterparts to adopt their parents' pattern of living. The bad news is that other research into how gay couples resolve conflicts showed that negotiation was very rarely used. A survey of 125 gay people, undertaken by CHEER (Centre for Homosexual Evaluation, Education and Research) found that while most of them considered that conflict was essential to their union (helping them clarify goals, values and rights), only 10 per cent of those interviewed could express anger and talk about the issues with their partners. The need of one to control the decisions and actions of the other was the main cause of conflict, followed closely by dependency (the need for one to lean on the other) and competition. Another study, conducted by John DeCecco and Michael Shively in 1975 concluded that "By avoiding negotiation, conflicts develop into serious breaks in relationships."

For most gay couples it will be a painful matter of trial and error before they find the most effective way to resolve differences between them, and if they can't find a satisfactory way of reaching agreement, then the whole relationship will be under threat. This is not to say that conflict should be avoided. Many people imagine that if they have arguments and rows with their loved ones, their relationship is a 'failure' or of 'poor quality'. Such people have been taken in by what psychologists call The Utopia Syndrome. As we all know, Utopia is a place where everything is perfection. Unfortunately, its other name is 'Nowhere'. Utopia doesn't exist, and neither does a conflict-free relationship. Those who claim that they never argue with their partner, never have shouting matches and never lose their temper are either lying or living in a relationship of unremitting boredom. Alternatively, they may *feel* the anger and resentment and frustration but never express it openly. They usually end up acting it out in other ways, by being late, getting drunk, throwing something or hitting out.

Being human, the end of our tether is sometimes reached and we end up having a screaming, shouting, all-barriers down row with our beloved. Such confrontations are inevitable and, according to one study of 200 couples, conducted by psychologist John Gottman, even desirable. Dr Gottman found that anger and disagreement are not harmful as long as they are not blended with wounding criticism. However, once the argument is over, a resolution to the problem has to be found. The fight may have got the issue that's troubling you onto the table, but it will take a different approach to sort it out. You have to find a more considered way of doing that.

One method worth thinking about is Formal Negotiation. We have given it this name because it does have a number of rules which must be accepted if it is to work. To most people, negotiation simply means working towards a mutually acceptable agreement and, to an extent, that definition is accurate. You may want to skip this chapter if you have no problems clearing up differences between you in such a way that neither feels resentful. If, on the other hand, joint decision-making leads to arguments, counter-arguments and eventually an all-out row, then you need to think about negotiation a bit more carefully. Mastering these skills at an early stage in the relationship will ensure that patterns of resentment and recrimination do not become fixed. Longer-established couples, too, might find that adapting this system might make their tried and tested methods more effective.

There doesn't have to be a winner and a loser in negotiations - indeed, if one partner cannot rest until he has won the day, then the rules need to be reconsidered and changes made. Both partners can win, although perhaps not always precisely the prize that had been sought. If one partner feels that he always has to back down in arguments or is always manipulated and overwhelmed in each discussion, then at some stage the resentment will make itself felt either directly or indirectly. In a healthy relationship both partners should feel that they are gaining something, that both have a fair share of the cake. Compromise is the key word here. If there is any sense of injustice, any feeling of exploitation, then something is wrong.

The reward for taking the trouble to master these relationship skills is a partnership which grows creatively, in which each partner feels safe, in which both participants can feel that their needs are heard and taken into account, even if they aren't always paramount. In short, a relationship which brings joy and happiness instead of conflict and misery.

It might take a conscious effort to realise that some of the means you use to get your own way could be destructive. It is sometimes an uncomfortable thing to sit down with your lover and listen to him pinpoint exactly what it is that you are doing which upsets him. No-one likes to think they are manipulative, domineering or insensitive to other people's feelings, but that might be the bottom line if you are in regular conflict with your partner. It is even more difficult, after having admitted these imperfections, to set about correcting them. However, that is exactly what you must do—together with your partner—if your partnership is to flourish and grow strong.

## Negotiation

Mastering the skill of negotiation will give your relationship one of its most precious assets. It can forestall the build up of resentments which get out of control and disintegrate into bitterness. If you work out mutually satisfactory conclusions to those petty (and not so petty) irritations, you can both feel free of exploitation. The feeling that you are put upon or taken for granted usually indicates that there is an area ripe for negotiation.

But negotiation in this context does not mean the same as, say, bargaining for a second-hand car. If you are trying to drive a hard bargain you will be out to get the best deal for yourself with little thought for the needs of the other party. A Machiavellian game of bluff and counter bluff might be played. If you manage to do your opponent down and have got the better end of the deal, then you will feel that you have won. In negotiating with your partner, however, you will be trying to ensure that you both end up winning something that is mutually satisfying. When you come away from a negotiation with your partner, neither of you should feel you have been taken for a ride, and neither should feel you have achieved a triumph at the other's expense. The idea is to improve your relationship, not overwhelm and subjugate your partner. Honesty is the answer, which is not always a straight-forward as it sounds.

In theory, gay relationships have a head start in negotiations; both partners are men and both will have been raised with the expectation that their needs are important. In straight couples there is often an assumed power structure in which the man's needs are seen as paramount; he earns the money, he rules the roost so he gets the lion's share in the decision-making. Of course, many women are challenging such assumptions, but there is still generally an imbalance. While such an unfair power structure may be less pronounced in a homosexual couple, there might be a clash of wills. Both may be strong characters, not used to emerging from negotiations on anything but the winning side. Perhaps both are used to hard negotiations as part of their job and think they can bring their ruthless business skills to their interpersonal negotiations (although these days even business negotiators try to employ the win-win philosophy in their dealings as they've found it more satisfactory as a long-term strategy). The aim is for both of you to get a fair amount of what you wanted. The sort of I-win-so-you-must-lose egotism has no part to play in negotiating with your loved one.

Being of the same sex doesn't necessarily mean that two people will be equally skilled in these kinds of discussions. If one partner is shy and retiring and not very good at asserting himself, then the other will have to make efforts not to take advantage of that to get his own way. If one partner feels hard done by after the negotiation is complete, then it has not succeeded.

Some of the issues on which negotiation can be carefully employed include: sex, money, lifestyles, holidays, careers and housework. There are a thousand other smaller topics which can be negotiated too.

Not everything needs to be formally negotiated, sometimes negotiating minor items may only take a few moments ("I'll do the cooking if you do the washing up. Agreed?"); but if there is an issue which cannot be resolved so easily ("How come your need to use the car always over-rides mine?") or some major and complex change of lifestyle ("I've been offered a year's contract in Tahiti and

I'd like you to give up your job and come with me.") then a formal negotiation might be called for.

Negotiations can only be successful if both partners are committed to making them work. If you read this section together, you should try to agree at the end of it that you'll both abide by the rules. If one of you is determined to get your own way, whatever the consequences, then there is little point in pretending that you are prepared to compromise, when all the time you are planning to use a steamroller. You should realise that trying to impose your will on your partner will only meet with resistance—direct or indirect—and create the kind of atmosphere which defeats the purpose of your relationship - which is to make you both feel secure and happy. If you persistently refuse to negotiate on an equal footing with your partner you might well be provoking a terminal confrontation.

When both partners feel that they are going into a negotiation with an equal opportunity to put their case and with no prospect of a power play being used on them, there is every chance of a successful conclusion.

When an issue arises that cannot be resolved by simple discussion, the time has come to call a formal negotiation. This might seem foolish, artificial and over-dramatic, but in fact it could save a great deal of pain, disagreement and bad feeling in the long run. Shouting matches and acrimonious confrontations might seem like a good way to release tension, and sometimes they are inevitable, but they can create more problems than they solve. Each time you have a blazing row in which one person becomes accusatory and the other defensive you simply draw further apart. Nothing gets settled, but more rancour is created, and there is only so much rancour that can be endured before questions about the value of a relationship are asked. Some people insist that they function best if they can shout and yell at each other. They say that the argument is over quickly and the anger isn't allowed to fester. If both partners can tolerate such fireworks (and most people would say that occasionally their temper snaps and they *have* to let rip) then that's fine. But such scenes rarely solve anything and after the shouting has died down, you still have to tackle the problem rationally.

So, why not ditch the old, bitter routines and try something more civilised? Negotiating so that you can both win means that you will both feel good instead of feeling distant from each other. Nobody has to back down and nobody has to crow about their triumph. Yes, it may all sound very contrived at first- it is! But as you become skilled in the techniques you will find that the need for a formal setting will diminish, you will find shortcuts for arriving at mutually acceptable decisions. Eventually formal negotiations with all the trappings will be needed only in the most contentious areas.

The first step is to ensure that the problem to be resolved has been properly identified. The partner who has called the negotiation, or who feels aggrieved, should write down the problem as briefly as possible, preferably in one sentence. An example might be: "I feel I am doing more than my fair share of housework and I'd like you to do more."

You can expand on this when the negotiation begins, perhaps telling your partner just how many tasks you perform in order to keep the house in a state fit to live in, and how much time it takes. Your partner should acknowledge that this is a problem, there should be no question of anyone saying: "I don't care how untidy the house gets, so it isn't a problem for me." If your partner feels badly about something in your relationship, then it is going to have an effect on your life together, and therefore it *is* your problem. Both partners should be friendly and calm. There should be no displays of bad temper, no huffing and puffing or shouting—hopefully you will have done your shouting and name-calling in the period before you decided to try and sort it out. If you aren't in the right frame of mind—perhaps because you're still angry about a shouting match you've had—then put the negotiation off until you've calmed down.

The next thing to do is to arrange the negotiation for a time and place when you will be uninterrupted. Turn off the television, take the phone off the hook and don't answer the doorbell. Give yourselves plenty of time to sort things out properly. There is nothing more frustrating than having to break off a negotiation and then try to pick up the threads again at another time. You might even choose a neutral setting for the negotiation, like a restaurant or park bench.

In industrial relations, skilled negotiators like to sit side by side at a table rather than facing each other. This can have an unconscious effect on how confrontational the meeting will be. Try to be on a level with each other - both either sitting or standing, not looking up or down at each other.

You need to communicate your needs to each other and there are several do's and don'ts to make this communication more effective.

- Don't say "never" or "always" in stating your views ("You never do anything around the house" or "I always get the dirty jobs"). It's unlikely to be true that your partner has never in his whole life contributed to the housework, and it is also unlikely that you always, without exception, do the dirty work.

153

- Make a pact that you will both start your sentences with "I" rather than "You". This will have a profound effect on how you express your worries. It will make sure you don't make your partner responsible for your own frustration. Don't say "You never tell me if you are going to be late home from work". Instead say: "I'd prefer if you told me if you are going to be late home from work."

- Don't say "should". What people "should" have done is usually only your opinion, and generally states the obvious anyway. ("You should be more careful when you're washing up, then there wouldn't be so many broken dishes.") If you use "should" on your partner you are turning him into a naughty child who doesn't know anything. You're bound to get a defensive reaction.

- Don't insult each other or use sarcasm, not even in jest. If you are negotiating about sex, don't start making wisecracks like "How can you have brewer's droop when you're a teetotaller?"

- Stick to the topic in hand. It's so easy to go off at a tangent, dragging in all kinds of irrelevant issues which are also bugging you. If there's something else you want to negotiate, leave it for a separate occasion.

- Don't rake up the past unless it is strictly relevant. You are trying to solve a problem which is present now and you don't want to keep digging things up that happened years ago as "proof" that your partner hasn't changed.

154

- Listen reflectively. This means you repeat in your own words the points that your partner is making. It ensures that you've understood what he's saying and reassures him that you're listening. But be careful that you don't change the sense of what he is saying so that it fits your own agenda. For instance, he might say: "I would really like us to spend Christmas at home this year, together, just the two of us" and you might say—under the guise of reflective listening—"You don't want to spend Christmas at my parents' home this year because you don't like them." That isn't what he said and probably isn't what he meant, either.

- Summarise each point as it is made. This helps clarify what exactly is being discussed and can help you see solutions.

- Use a soft, loving and affectionate tone of voice, accompanied by non-threatening body language. A smile, eye contact, sitting close together, even holding hands can reassure your partner that he is safe to really get the heart of the problem. Don't shout, cry, sneer or mock. Body language which can ruin a negotiation include rolling eyes upwards, frowning, jabbing finger, sitting distantly, folding arms and turning away.

- Don't interrupt each other. When you cut your partner off mid-sentence, the hidden message is: 'I don't really want to listen to you - you have nothing of interest to say.'

Some partners who use negotiation (and I heartily recommend it for anyone who is serious about making their relationship work) go to the trouble of researching their problem before they start. For instance, if you can't agree about where to go for your annual holiday and decide to negotiate formally, then both partners can prepare their case in advance. Should one of you think that a skiing holiday would be great while the other longs for a beach holiday in the sun, then the time has come to talk it through. Before you start, both of you could draw up a list of pros and cons for each destination, and any other solution which you can think of for the dilemma. For instance, would it be possible to have a two-centre holiday, one week at a beach resort and the other week skiing? Is it possible that this year you'll take separate holidays? Maybe it would be acceptable if you both agreed to go skiing this year and beach resorting next year. As you can see, here are a number of possible solutions and if both partners can agree to one of them, they can both come away feeling they've got something which is acceptable.

The success of this depends of whether the partners have entered the negotiation with the intention of compromising on their original demand. Its success also depends on whether partners intend to abide by what has been agreed. It would be unfair in the extreme to agree to a skiing holiday this year and beach next and then conveniently 'forget' the arrangement the following summer. That is why it is important to write down the conclusion. Make sure you both understand what you've decided and that you both accept it.

It might seem like a lot of effort, but in fact it doesn't take long to write down ideas for discussion. The process of formalised thinking can itself actually produce a satisfactory solution which would otherwise not have been considered. Surely this is better than the alternative of fighting, arguing and feeling bad because neither of you will give an inch.

Some people will feel threatened if they can't keep control of a situation. If they feel they've got to compromise something that is important to them, they might become angry, frightened and defensive. If this happens to you during a negotiation then you will need to take a step back and think about what you are doing and why. Go over the specific problem again with your partner and try to bear in mind that you cannot have a satisfying relationship if either of you insist on unilateral control.

There are other ways in which partners might unthinkingly try to get their own way. Cajoling and threatening are two: neither is acceptable in the negotiation.

Imagination should be employed, too, in making your decision. If you are trying to work out who does what jobs in the house then a straight fifty-fifty split of chores is unlikely to be equitable. Some jobs are more pleasant than others, some take longer and need more effort and skill. What about awarding varying numbers of points to each job according to its unpleasantness, time or energy consumption and so on? Therefore, walking the dog might score 1, while cleaning the lavatory might merit 5; doing the shopping could rate 6, because it takes a long time and much effort. Vacuuming on the other hand might only be 2.

When you've apportioned the jobs according to their points value (and taking into account other factors such as one person being a more enthusiastic cook than the other, and therefore volunteering to prepare all the meals, or one person having much more free time than the other), you might also want to decide when and how often these jobs are to be done. You could also have a rota where you swap tasks on a weekly or monthly basis.

After you've come to a satisfactory conclusion, write it all down and ensure that you both understand what tasks are whose responsibility and when they will be performed. If either of you flouts the agreement, then it needs to be reviewed and another system tried.

Naturally you shouldn't be too inflexible; there will be times when one partner won't be able to pull his weight in the house; maybe he's ill or under intense pressure at work or having trouble with his family. If you love him, you'll know when to make allowances and you'll do it gladly. Perhaps one partner actually enjoys housework and keeping the home neat and clean. In that case, no negotiation is needed. The situation might change, and the option to negotiate must always be kept open.

When two people get together to form an emotional partnership there are a thousand and one decisions to make. Mostly the couple will be able to come to some amicable arrangement without a lot of hassle, but on these occasions when disagreements occur and anger flourishes, negotiations can be a god-send.

## Tolerance

If your partner has some great enthusiasm in his life which you don't share—travelling, antique collecting, model trains or astronomy or whatever—you have a couple of options. One is to negotiate with his so that his other great love doesn't take over his life to your exclusion ("I know you love hang gliding, but do you think you could come down to earth long enough for us to talk about it?"). If you feel you don't want to get involved with your partner's hobby, then work out between you how you are going to spend some of your leisure time together. After all, part of the reason you got into this relationship was for the companionship!

Tolerance is the key word here. People who are fanatics about something can be a bore, but they can also be extremely stimulating. Having a partner who is so interested in something that he embraces aspects of it with great gusto is surely better than having one who sits in front of the TV set every evening. If you can't share his interest, then at least try to tolerate and accommodate it. You'll earn his love and appreciation for not trying to dilute his enjoyment of something which means so much to him.

# Chapter Eight:
# Jealousy

It has been said that if a lover feels no jealousy he doesn't feel love either, but the anthropologist Margaret Mead argued the opposite, saying: "Jealousy is not a barometer by which depths of love can be read, but merely records the degree of the lover's insecurity."

Jealousy is indeed one of the most destructive powers that can be released in a relationship and hardly any long-term partnership runs its course without the intrusion of the green-eyed monster. For some people it is a mild and manageable phenomenon, for others it can become an all-consuming and crippling obsession.

Dr Debora Phillips, an American psychiatrist, defines jealousy as: "a parasite that feeds on love. You know it makes you selfish, possessive, anxious and repulsive - full of hate anger and suspicion. You know it makes you an ugly pawn to its demands. And you know that just feeling

160

the emotions is a dead end trap that damages what you want most." So, where does jealousy come from and how can we deal with it?

When we talk about jealousy we usually mean the sexual kind - we are afraid that our partner has found a new lover. This suspicion, which may or may not have a basis in reality, produces all kinds of pain and discomfort for the sufferer; it can led to undignified behaviour and destructive confrontations. It can change form during the lifetime of a long-term relationship: in the early days it is likely to be pure sexual jealousy of the kind which causes you to say: "I can't bear the idea of my lover having sex with someone else." Later the sexual possessiveness might lessen and jealousy is more likely to express a fear of losing the relationship. "I don't mind you playing around, but I'm afraid that one day you'll find someone who will take you away from me."

Then there is jealousy's close companion, envy. If one partner is doing better than the other in his career on some other sphere of life, envy can lead to resentment and fearsome competition which will, in the end, escalate into destruction. This kind of envy usually springs from the fear of change. If one partner finds his career is taking off, while the other's is in the doldrums, there can be a sense of threat for the partner lagging behind. As his confidence dwindles, his more successful partner seems to be going from strength to strength. A jobless partner, whose self-esteem is probably at a low ebb, might begin to imagine that, with his new-found success, his lover will want to move on to "better things" in his emotional life, too. A lot of reassurance is needed here, and a carefully thought-out plan to get the floundering partner back on the move.

161

## Making Gay Relationships Work

Once depression sets in it can be very difficult to shift. So however busy and in-demand you might be, always try to be aware of your partner's moods and needs; he might be falling into a spiral of discouragement. You will want to help him anyway; but not doing so may also affect your relationship adversely. If he begins to show envy of your success, then it's likely he feels threatened by it; he probably feels that he is going to lose you just as he feels he's losing himself.

It's common for men to define themselves by their job ("I'm a plumber or doctor or social worker or bus driver") and if they should lose that job they might feel they've lost a key part—if not the whole—of their identity. But most of us have ups and downs in our careers and when we're in a rut it's not always easy to appreciate that there will be other opportunities. One of the great things about being in a partnership is that lovers can support each other through these low points and hopefully demonstrate that they're rooting for each other. If you partner knows that you love is constant and not dependent on his career-showing, you can avoid much of the envy that changing fortunes at work might provoke.

### Sexual Jealousy

When heterosexuals get married, part of the vow they take is to be sexually faithful. Although very often this vow is not kept, at least the husband and wife are aware of the initial ground rules. Gay relationships don't start out with any such automatic commitment or assumption; most gay couples will have to work out their own attitudes to monogamy. Unfortunately, many don't, and the crisis that can follow when monogamy is breached can be a real threat to the relationship. Perhaps they don't discuss the topic because they are afraid of it, maybe they feel embarrassed to raise it in case their partner thinks they are trying to impose unreasonable restrictions.

If you haven't sorted out your attitudes to sexual exclusivity, then you should make an effort to do so. It can help you both avoid hurt feelings and relationship-threatening misunderstandings. Don't assume your partner "knows" how you feel if you haven't discussed it - nor should you assume that he agrees with your feelings if he hasn't said so directly. If both partners know where they stand, and trust each other to keep commitments they have agreed to, then problems can be minimised.

But human relationships aren't as simple as that, and human beings are prone to changing needs. Maybe over a period of time one partner is finding it difficult to keep a promise of monogamy. Perhaps someone else has come along who will provide a temporary sexual release, or an opportunity for some other outside sexual activity presents itself and is not resisted. Several researchers into male homosexual relationships have discovered that by the end of the second year a renewed interest in outside sexual contact often materialises. Because both men have been socially conditioned to the male role, it is likely that they will subscribe to the double standard often found in marriages: "It's OK for me to play around because I know I can keep my dalliances under control—it's just sex—but the idea of her doing it with someone else makes me feel jealous and threatened." And so both partners in a gay relationship might think it OK for them the enjoy sexual contact outside the relationship, but still feel threatened by their lover's sexual adventurings. Naturally with Aids becoming increasingly an issue for gay men there are other considerations to take into account. Can partners trust each other to have only safer sex with casual contacts away from the primary relationship? Will knowledge of other sexual contacts create a fear of disease which will interfere with the functioning of the primary relationship? Common sense (as well as Aids organisations) tells us that the more sexual contacts we have, the greater the likelihood of being exposed to HIV. Obviously only the safest of safer sex is acceptable between casual partners.

For safety's sake, more and more gay couples are trying to opt for monogamy. However, if primary partners are cheating on one another (and if a promise of monogamy has been made and not kept, then cheating is the right word), the whole relationship is being undermined. If your partner can't trust you to keep this mutually agreed commitment, can he trust you to keep any other?

Many gay couples change their attitudes towards monogamy as their relationship progresses. Some research shows that most committed gay couples are respectful of each other's needs in this area, and they work out rules which will save conflict. Some have decided that even though they are prepared to accept each other's sexual dalliances outside the primary relationship, there must be hard and fast rules about how these extra-relationship affairs will be conducted. For instance, some couples insist that if they go out together, they will come back together. There will be no flirting with other people in front of each other. Other couples have decided that any outside activity must be 'just sex' with no emotional attachments. If they see other people it must only be once or maybe twice. Some insist that no outside sexual partners should be brought home or that they will tolerate other partners only when on holiday abroad - where they can pose no threat to home life. Andy and Joe experienced a similar change in attitudes:

"When we first started living together—and for the first three years or so afterwards—I thought that being faithful was the most important thing in the world," said Andy. "I was so much in love with Joe I couldn't tolerate the idea of him going off with other people. And I didn't want to go off with anyone either. I felt in the early days that it would have tainted something wonderful. But gradually our sex life together didn't seem like enough, and we both started looking at other people again as possible sex partners. Not that either of us spent much time seeking out other men for sex - it was just when something special came along, or when there was an opportunity to have a bit of fun on the side. The first time I went off with another man was after a party I'd gone to alone, and I felt very guilty about it, as though I'd betrayed Joe in some way. All the time I was having sex with this other man I kept thinking about Joe and wondering if he would be hurt. I hoped he wouldn't find out about it, but he did. I was surprised he wasn't more angry, but he just accepted it, and we agreed that if either of us was going to have sex with other partners, we wouldn't tease each other about it. It never really posed any threat to our relationship, and Joe and I feel close enough to each other now to know that we are the most important people in the world to each other. Our security was never threatened by having flings with other people, even when they lasted several months and were quite

165

intense. Many of the contacts we have made in this way have since gone on to become mutual friends. We tried a threesome once, but neither of us liked it very much. Otherwise we don't seem to get desperately jealous – just the occasional twinge if I think I'm being neglected. Even so, we try very hard to keep our home very much just for the two of us, and we never bring lovers back there to have sex. I'm much more wary of who I go off with these days and what I do with them."

Andy and Joe still have sex with each other several times a month and since Aids became an issue, their outside contacts have diminished considerably. They are both aware of the dangers of unprotected sex. "To be honest with you," says Joe, "I'm scared stiff—and sometimes scared limp—of picking up HIV. I simply don't enjoy sex with people I don't know very well any more. The fantasy is much better than the reality. There's always a sort of unpleasant tension about it. I'm very pleased I've got Andy."

Andy and Joe showed good sense in acknowledging the change in their relationship, and ensuring that they both understood the new terms. Although Andy was the first to break the unspoken agreement that they would be monogamous, they managed between them to negotiate a new arrangement without too much friction. This is not always the case.

## Keeping Agreements

Let's assume that you have negotiated an arrangement that is acceptable to both of you. If the agreement is that you will be sexually exclusive, then you should try very hard not to abuse the trust that your partner has invested in you. If trust, that most essential ingredient of a successful relationship, is to be maintained it must be accorded every respect. You cannot pick and choose the issues on which you will be serious about the bond of trust you have established. If you feel you cannot keep a promise, then it is important that you go back to your partner and negotiate rather than betray. Naturally if there has been a trivial incident, which happened spontaneously and without forethought, and which has no other meaning for you (perhaps you had a fleeting, but safe, anonymous sexual adventure when out jogging), then you might feel that less hurt would be caused by keeping it to yourself. But if a secondary relationship has begun which will require premeditated lying and much deception in order to maintain, then you must think very carefully about the consequences. Trust is so important between you that it cannot be seriously compromised without risking dire consequences on the whole relationship.

Like Andy and Joe, some couples agree that they will allow each other to have outside sexual partners, but usually there are conditions attached. Maybe your partner says it's OK for you to play around as long as you don't let him know it is happening, or maybe he feels better if he does know what's going on. Maybe you will agree on certain times of the week when you will allow each other to go out and 'cruise', so long as it doesn't impinge on your other important times together. Perhaps the condition says that neither of you will bring other partners to your home, or that you will not have sex with mutual friends. Once again, a condition which is fundamental and should not be open to negotiation is that only the safest of safer sex will be practised with casual sexual partners.

167

Even when partners start out with a relationship that is ostensibly 'open', they might discover that in practice it is less easily coped with. Jealousy is not a respecter of decisions made in the cold light of day. One partner might find his partner's non-monogamy more difficult to accept on an emotional level than on an intellectual one. The feelings that go with jealousy are extremely unpleasant, sometimes they can be so violent as to resemble a physical illness.

Much has been written about jealousy, and it seems to be a universal emotion. The theory that it is the expression of paranoid insecurity has been countered by the idea that it is an age-old instinct which helped out primitive ancestors hold on to their hard-won mates. Whichever theory is correct, there is no doubt that jealousy is a real and potent force.

There are two kinds of sexual jealousy, the kind that springs from reality, when there is indisputable proof that the partner is finding sexual contact outside the relationship (reality-based jealousy); and the kind that springs from the suspicion and insecurity of the sufferer and has no basis in actual events (paranoid jealousy).

When you know that your partner is seeing someone else for sex then it is reasonable, if it is causing you distress, to talk about it with him. If you have agreed that it will be OK for him to have other partners, but then find you can't cope with it, then tell him so. The time has come for a renegotiation. Follow the procedure as for any other negotiation which is explained in the chapter on Relationship Skills. It goes without saying that this issue is potentially more explosive than others, so care must be taken to keep calm, be rational and follow the rules. If you are seething with anger and furious at having been betrayed, then ensure that you make your partner very much aware of this. But any screaming and shouting which needs to be done should be done away from the negotiation.

You and your partner are going to have to do some hard talking about trust in your relationship following any breach of agreement. Having said that, it must be acknowledged that gay men generally find minor 'indiscretions' in their partner to be of little consequence and have no problem in simply ignoring or accepting them. They recognise how easy it is to have a little fling and how many opportunities there are to do so. Jealousy in such cases can be fleeting and quickly be rationalised out of existence.

## When It Becomes A Problem

This all sounds very cool and simple, but it isn't always so. Jealousy can release passions of such intensity that confrontations about it can rapidly lead the relationship into taking a final nose-dive. Release the anger by all means, but try to do it in a controlled and constructive way and give yourself time to recover.

The temptation in some instances is to walk out of the relationship there and then. Don't do it. More bad decisions have been made in the heat of a jealous rage than at almost any other time. By all means have some time to yourself to think it over–staying temporarily with a friend if you want time and space to consider the future. But *do not make any irrevocable decisions at this point*. And let your partner know what you are doing and why.

You may well imagine that you will never forgive your partner if he had sworn to keep your love exclusive and then discover that he hasn't done so, but you will also discover that time will bring a more reasonable frame of mind. I have met several men who have been desperately hurt by their partners' broken promises, and ended the relationship immediately they found out. Months later they expressed deep regret at their impetuous decision. Most managed to patch up the relationship and go back with a clearer understanding of what was expected, others found that it had been damaged beyond repair.

Of course, jealousy can show itself in different ways. Sometimes partners living in 'open' relationships find that one person is making more use of the privilege than the other; some gay men are better at cruising or cottaging than others: they have a more easy-going approach and can take rejection more lightly. They may also be more physically attractive than their partners. So, if both partners have agreed that extra-relationship sex will be permitted, it might turn out that one is having a whale of a time while the other (because of shyness, lack of success at picking up partners, or lack of desire to do so) feels lonely and a failure. Soon resentment about frequent nights out on the tiles begins to surface. The less successful lover begins to feel annoyed about his partner's activities, his confidence diminishes as he sits at home, alone watching television and feeling increasingly jealous. It might all have seemed fine when he agreed to it, but not so wonderful when it actually happens. In situations like that, a renegotiation is called for. If one partner feels strongly that he needs outside sexual activity, while the other has strong reservations about it, it can be a painful and prolonged negotiation. However, if you are determined to sort it out in a way that is satisfactory to both of you, then follow the rules for negotiation and be particularly aware of trying to manipulate each other. The partner who wants sex outside the relationship might try to make his lover feel guilty about trying to restrict him, while the other partner might try to swing the negotiation in his favour by rationalising the jealousy and issuing threats about ending the relationship. It's an area fraught with difficulties, and if there can be no genuine agreement then your whole future together might be at risk.

## Is There A Positive Side To Jealousy?

Some people will argue that jealousy is also a positive emotion, a good indicator that the relationship has not become moribund. Relationship therapist, Dr Robin Skynner has written that we should recognise that jealousy has a potential for "facilitating confidence and autonomy and generating pleasurable excitement". He also says: "I would be pleased to have as many hot dinners as I have seen couples where discovery of a brief infidelity has fanned the dying embers of their sexual relationship, or brought it to life for the first time."

There is no doubt that an outside sexual encounter can create a new dynamism in a relationship, and many gay couples have reported that their sex life with their primary partner was revived after they had a "fling" with someone else.

## Paranoid Jealousy

The other kind of jealousy is the paranoid, suspicious kind that has no reality outside the imagination of the sufferer, who feels sure that his lover is playing around at every opportunity. If your partner is late home from work, your jealous mind might go into overdrive. Why is he staying so late at the office, you might ask yourself. Maybe it has something to do with that new accounts clerk who started last week and whom your lover described as "quite humpy". Suppose they found the attraction mutual, you think. Suppose they've decided to take it further. What if they are, at this very moment, sprawled over your lover's desk in his locked office, having hot sex? The later it gets and the more complex the scenario becomes. Maybe they are falling in love! Suppose your lover is finding this new man more interesting, more stimulating, more sexy than you. Immediately the dreadful sensations that go with jealousy materialise: the heavy feeling in the pit of the stomach, the nausea, the panic, the anxiety.

You can't rest for your imaginings. The second hand of the kitchen clock seems to be operating slow motion. You pace up and down, peeping through the curtains at two minute intervals to see if his car is in the drive. Why doesn't he ring? What are they doing now?

When he comes home you react in one of two ways: you either fly at him making all kinds of wild accusations or you become sullen, quiet and uncommunicative. In some ways the first reaction is preferable. If you sulk he will sit there wondering what on earth he can have done to deserve this treatment. "What's the matter?" he asks, and you reply: "Nothing", but continue to treat him to the unexplained silence.

As he tries to break the atmosphere by telling you what he's been doing today (casually mentioning that the humpy new clerk went off on his honeymoon at the weekend), you realise your fears were unfounded, that he was telling the truth about the sudden rush of work at the office, and you begin to unwind a little. You know you've been irrational, and that you've inflicted torture upon yourself, and eventually you allow yourself to forget the incident - until next time, of course, when the whole thing starts again.

Paranoid jealousy can lead to all kinds of undignified behaviour. A friend of mine would listen in on the extension to telephone conversations and steam open any hand-written letters which were addressed to his lover. Every little deviation from the routine would trigger the feelings of jealousy. No amount of reassurance from his lover made any difference. He certainly felt better while these reassurances were being given, but it didn't last long - he just simply couldn't shake off the feelings of jealousy.

## Dealing With Paranoid Jealousy

If you have a partner who displays the symptoms of paranoid jealousy, you will find that there is little you can do to reassure him. However much you tell him that you love him, respect him, find him attractive and so on, it will have little effect. Jealousy overwhelms all such reassurances. It is now up to the jealous partner to recognise that the problem is his, and begin to work on it.

For the insecure person the order to "increase self-esteem" is a tall one, but it is really the only long-term solution. You could start the process by finding a therapist who can help you confront the problem and find ways of easing it. Such an effort and investment would be surely worthwhile if it would help rid you of the terrible torment which is jealousy. Another positive step you can take is to increase your own social life in as many ways as you can. Having a life away from your partner (as well as enjoying the one you share) takes away the dependency that can easily build up when one partner is lacking in confidence. If you feel you rely almost completely on your partner for your social life, then you will tend to be anxious when he is not around - and especially if you imagine he is playing the field. Having your own circle of friends, who will support you and offer you alternative social outlets, is always a good idea. You will both benefit from not expecting your partner to provide all social outlets.

Having your honesty, loyalty and love constantly questioned is not a pleasant experience. Even the most tolerant and understanding of partners will eventually become impatient with a jealous lover. By placing such pressure on a partner, paranoid jealousy can bring about directly the very circumstance the sufferer fears most - the end of the relationship.

So, even if you know that you feel jealous, and can't control the feelings, try to keep quiet about them until you have evidence that they have a basis in reality. Leave suspicion unspoken until you are sure. It might mean torment for you, but at least it will keep the pressure off your partner.

## The Value Of Relaxation

Another useful self-help technique is relaxation. When you are suffering from these dreadful feelings of jealousy your anxiety level increases substantially. Anxiety and relaxation are incompatible, so if you can learn to relax yourself, empty your mind of fear-inducing thoughts, you can relieve many of the symptoms that go with paranoid jealousy.

The first thing to do is master a relaxation technique. The progressive tense-relax system (also called deep muscle relaxation) is probably best for this purpose. Choose the quietest room and, if possible, a time when you know you won't be interrupted. Tell your partner, if he's around, or leave a 'do not disturb' sign on the door. Turn off the phone, find yourself a comfortable chair or for preference, lay on the floor and close your eyes. Take a deep breath and allow yourself to exhale slowly. Take another deep breath and exhale again. Now make a fist with your left hand, squeezing it as tight as you can. Notice the tension in your hand as you do this and after ten seconds let the tension go and relax your hand. Repeat this. Do the same thing with your right hand. Then flex your left arm as hard as you can, feeling the tension in the muscles of your forearm and upper arm. After ten seconds allow it to relax. Repeat. Do the same with the other arm. Then hunch your shoulders, pulling them up as high as you can, hold for ten seconds and relax. Repeat. Then lift your head off the ground, putting your chin as near to your chest as you can get it. Then relax your neck and rest your head on the floor again. Repeat. Screw up your face as hard as you can, feeling the tension around your nose, mouth and forehead. Relax. Repeat. Then repeat the tense/relax routine with all the other muscle groups in your body: legs, buttocks, feet, abdomen and so on. Work on each area of your body until they are all relaxed. Then clear your mind of all thoughts and focus it on one particular tranquil and pleasing image (which has nothing to do with your partner) or a word which you can repeat to yourself as a sort of chant.

When you are feeling anxious because of jealousy (or for any other reason), you can relax yourself using this technique, and relieve many of the troubling feelings which are bothering you. By replacing the fantasies which cause the jealousy with agreeable sensations of deep relaxation you can eventually learn to keep it under control. The feelings that go with jealousy are, of course, very strong and persistent, and it will take a lot of practice before you can learn to dispel them from your mind with this effort of will. So keep on trying.

There are several excellent audio tapes that will talk you through the relaxation process and if you find it hard to manage on your own, then an investment in one of these tapes will be money well spent.

Reinforce your determination to change by telling yourself (when you are calm and not feeling jealous) that your jealous spells are not based on reality and that they are self-inflicted. Rationalise your feelings when you are free of them and they will have less power over you next time they materialise.

## Power Play

Jealousy can also be used as a means for one partner to exercise power over the other. It is not unknown for one partner to play on the other's insecurity by flirting or threatening sexual encounters outside the relationship. The resultant anxiety can give a spurious advantage to the tormentor during negotiations, but such cruel manipulation has no place in a loving relationship; it hurts the person we are trying to love and that is not healthy. These kinds of power games are often played subconsciously and can be difficult to pinpoint. However, if you feel your partner uses such ploys to get his own way in your relationship, or if you recognise that you do this to your lover, then identify the manipulation and work towards eliminating it.

## Possessiveness

Another aspect of jealousy is possessiveness. It means that the jealous person demands full and undivided attention from his partner. When he is left alone such a person feels almost like an abandoned child, on the verge of being unable to function as an autonomous human being. He needs to feel that he is loved every minute of the day, and that love must be proved constantly.

Such clinging behaviour imposes and enormous strain on the relationship. If the possessive person's lover pays attention to anyone else, even in the most innocent way, he will intervene and demand that the spotlight be turned on him. Accusations will be made about disloyalty if attention flags for even a moment. He will track his lover's movements closely and obsessively check his whereabouts.

Once again, all this springs from a conviction in the sufferer that he has no value as an individual. The constant reassurances offered by his lover have no lasting effect on his feeling of inferiority. A lot of work needs to be done by such an individual to conquer these feelings, to rationalise them, to accept them as a failing and get them under control. A counsellor might be the first step.

Again, increased self-esteem is the answer, but that comes from so many other things. Challenge yourself to achieve something new and work to make that challenge come true. On the way you will increase your sense of self-worth. Accept that even if you don't succeed in every particular of your challenge you have at least had a go. Don't punish yourself as a failure if you only get part of the way. Every time you succeed, you will feel better about yourself.

Whether your challenge is a new job, learning another language, going back to some kind of education or maybe improving your cooking skills, tackling it will help your confidence. Doing is the only answer. Thinking about doing but remaining passive is self-defeating. If you make some friends along the way, so much the better. A rich social life of your own is another way to loosen the grip of possessiveness.

Don't expect overnight results from any of these suggestions. Once you have recognised the problem you can tackle it, but you will need patience and determination to put things right.

The good news is that jealousy tends to diminish the longer a relationship lasts. As partners become more confident in each other and as their individual selves re-emerge after a period of suppression, jealousy loses much of its power. It is unlikely to be conquered completely (and if it is, then maybe it is because the partners have grown indifferent to each other, which is far worse) but gay couples of many years' standing often find that as time passes they are better able to control jealousy and neutralise its destructive effects.

# Chapter Nine:

# Sex

In the old days (not so long ago) when sex was more strictly controlled, the agony columns of women's magazines were inundated with letters from apprehensive brides-to-be, anxious to know what was expected of them on their wedding night. In those days, nice girls didn't go 'all the way' before marriage, and knowledge of sex was a closed book for many women and men. Fortunately, with the advent of reliable contraception, pre-marital sex doesn't carry the same taboo, and young people tend to regard love-making as an enjoyable pastime rather than a source of shame.

Gay relationships nearly always start with a sexual encounter and then develop or fizzle out from there. However, this preliminary emphasis on sex doesn't mean that all issues connected with it will have been resolved or even discussed before serious thought is given to establishing a partnership.

As we've observed before, within a relationship the libido is at its most active during the honeymoon period. The freshness of the sex, the new body to explore, the novel ideas that are introduced, all these things got to ensure that interest doesn't flag for the first few months or maybe even years. But after that, you come to recognise that unless you make an effort your sex life together can easily fall into a rut, become boring and eventually cause you to take each other for granted.

Sex, like any other skill, needs practice and imagination to keep it exciting. If you find that you are not getting much of a thrill from your sexual encounters with your partner, and that anticipating them doesn't excite you any more, then you've probably come to see sex as something you do to relieve the occasional randy feelings or as a duty to please your partner. When that point is reached, your sex life can rapidly become little more than an extension of your masturbatory life, a simple release from sexual pressure.

If routine has set in, boredom will surely follow, and partners can find they are doing the same old thing time after time, without thought and sometimes without feeling, but often with resentment. It's rather like having jut one recipe in your culinary repertoire. If you eat the same dish for every meal, you'll soon get tired of it and start thinking about going out to a restaurant. The alternative, of course, is to learn a few new dishes and vary the menu, in that way the urge to sample other people's fare is lessened.

You have to be equally creative and innovative with your sexual life together. If either of you feel that your sexual encounters have become humdrum, then it's time to start thinking of ways to change.

The first stumbling block here is actually broaching the subject, and the second is making suggestions for improvement. It's a strange anomaly in human relationships that while we might be prepared to do all kinds of exotic things in bed with our partner, we often have great difficulty talking about those activities. When you're carried away in sexual ecstasy, inhibitions can miraculously disappear but afterwards when things have calmed down, you might find that trying to analyse what you've just done brings on a fit of cringing embarrassment. The image of sitting in bed, having a post-coital cigarette and asking "How was it for you?" has become a joke because for so many people it wasn't much at all. And few people are going to offer up a blow-by-blow account of what they liked and what they didn't like. Can you imagine it? "It was lovely darling, but next time I'd prefer only one finger up my arse rather than two." However useful that information might be for a lover, it is extremely difficult to articulate.

But asking the question "How was it for you?" in a loving and constructive way might be the only way of getting things moving again.

Sex is the hardest thing to negotiate: so much of our self-image is bound up in this most intimate act. When we make love we are exposing our psyche in a way that we hardly ever do in other aspects of life: one cutting remark, one inappropriate laugh and an erection can disappear in a couple of seconds, taking with it a lot of the owner's self-confidence.

Because of the unique trust that sex entails, it is an area that gives us the greatest opportunity to express our special love for our partner. It also gives us the greatest power to hurt. If you want your relationship to grow and be mutually joyous never, never use that special vulnerability which goes with sex as a means of manipulation. If you do so, you risk ruining something that could bring you great happiness.

So, in negotiating about sexual matters a special sensitivity is required. It would be hurtful indeed if you approached such a negotiation by saying: "You're a lousy lover. Sex with you is about as exciting as watching paint dry." That may be what you think, but if your partner lacks self-esteem in this area or if he is under the impression that your sex life is OK, he might be dreadfully hurt to hear you say such a thing. On the other hand, a more diplomatic approach ("I love you dearly, but there's something I'd like to discuss. I think we're getting into a bit of a rut with our sex life. Is it OK to talk?") might well make your partner realise that he, too, hasn't been getting as much he could from your encounters. It's a minefield but it doesn't mean you shouldn't try to cross it. Pre-existing goodwill and trust can make it safer and less painful for all concerned.

In the past when gay partners found sexual interest in their primary partner beginning to diminish, they have turned to others for sexual refreshment. Because of the invisible presence of HIV this is not quite the uncomplicated pleasure it once was, and has led gay couples to try harder to find ways to keep their primary sexual partner fresh and exciting.

Communication is all-important to achieve a more lasting interest. If he isn't giving you all you want, why not tell him what it is you like to do. If you particularly like oral sex, for instance, and he isn't giving it to you, then ask how he feels about it. It may be that he's been too shy to suggest it and has been waiting for you to take the initiative. Or maybe you don't need to say anything, just move his head or his hand to the area that particularly turns you on. If you can't bring yourself to say what you like, try demonstrating to him when he reaches the relevant places by groaning and making other encouraging noises. Be careful, though, as

182

non-verbal signals can be misinterpreted; what you hoped sounded like a yelp of pleasure might make your partner feel that he is hurting you. Look at pornography together, and when you see things that particularly appeal to you, let your partner know that you'd like to try them.

Feeling shy about some of your sexual desires, and keeping them secret is a common human reaction. We may fantasise about particular sexual activities, and long to try them, but be afraid to tell our lover in case he disapproves or is shocked ("I sometimes fantasise about my previous boyfriend when I'm having sex with my present lover"). On the other hand, these secrets may represent major traumas ("My grandfather fucked me just about every night when I was a child"). Guilty feelings about our sexual secrets makes it difficult to share them with our lover. We may fear that if we told him what is going on in our head or what has happened to us in the past, he might be repulsed or rejecting.

Errol and Dean have been lovers for two years. Errol longs to tell Dean that he is increasingly attracted to the idea of S&M. He wants to try it to see whether it would live up to his fantasies. He'd love Dean to spank him and treat him roughly during sex, but can't tell Dean about these desires because he is afraid of rejection.

"Dean is fairly adventurous sexually, but he has never expressed any interest in S&M. He always says people have the right to do whatever turns them on, but he has never said that it turns *him* on. I feel that if I tell him that I secretly yearn to be spanked and held down he will be horrified and go off me. I would feel very ashamed if he reacted

> badly to the suggestion. So I keep it to myself and
> feel deprived."

This sexual secret is creating a barrier between the two of them, and is affecting the sex life that they do have. Errol now feels that their lovemaking is repetitive, and he goes through the motions to please Dean, while feeling vaguely resentful that he hasn't got what he wants.

Errol knows that Dean is not really the 'shockable' type. They've talked about most things together, and Dean has never shown any prudish tendencies. But still Errol is reluctant to broach the subject of mild S&M in their own sex life, so afraid is he of rejection.

Tony experienced something similar with his partner Piers:

> "When we were on holiday, Piers and I made mad, passionate love in a hotel room that with a large mirror on the wall. As Piers made love to me, I was able to watch the whole thing in this mirror. I found it an incredible turn-on, although Piers didn't seem to notice it. When we got back home I was hot to repeat the experience, but I was worried that Piers would think I was pervy. We could easily have brought the big mirror up from the living room into the bedroom and position it so that we could see all the action. I just can't tell him that I'd like to do it."

It's amazing how many people feel that they could cope with hearing their partner's sexual secrets, but don't think their partner could handle hearing theirs. The truth is that partner's probably won't be shocked, and some of them might even be intrigued or pleased at the suggestion. If the both partners are keeping their secret desires from each other, then their sexual life together is likely to quickly deteriorate as neither gets what they really want.

The secret, however, may be something much more painful, such as memories of childhood sexual abuse. If you are keeping such secrets from your partner and feel that it is interfering with your life together, it may be worth contacting one of the incest survivors groups for counselling. Trusting your partner enough to share these secrets sometimes means taking a risk. In most instances, it's a risk worth taking. The *worry* about bad reactions will probably be quite out of proportion to the reality.

## What is Faithful?

Sex doesn't always have to be restricted to the same person, of course. Research has shown that most participants in gay relationships have sex outside of their primary relationship at some stage - one survey discovered that after five years not a single one of their study sample of 150 gay couples had remained monogamous. Another (admittedly conducted pre-Aids) put the proportion at 73%. This illustrates one of the main differences between gay and straight relationships. Gay couples generally put far less emphasis on sexual fidelity than their straight counterparts. Indeed, being 'faithful' in a gay relationship has a far wider meaning than it does for heterosexuals. Having a fling with someone other than your partner doesn't necessarily mean the death of the relationship, or even a serious threat to it. Dishonesty, lack of concern, manipulation - these are the issues which gay couples may consider far more important than sexual exclusivity.

## Making Gay Relationships Work

This is not to say that jealousy plays no part. However liberated and 'open' a couple might be, they can never be sure that they are not going to be the victims of jealousy. These are issues which each couple must come to terms with according to their own needs and feelings. If sexual monogamy is important to you and your partner, then that is fine. But if extra-relationship sex is a need, and both agree, then it should also be possible to incorporate it. Both formulas have been shown to work for gay men. Don't let anybody convince you that there is a 'correct' way of doing things - each couple must make its own rules.

### Incompatibility Versus Patience

Incompatibility is a word bandied about a great deal by people who are having sexual difficulties, but it is often introduced into the proceedings at far too early a stage. The sexual chemistry which can spark between two people might be immediate or it might need a little patience and experimentation. This was certainly the case with Bob and Nigel. They met at a night club, fancied each other and went home together. It soon became clear that Bob was by far the most sexually experienced of the two, and found he was taking most of the initiatives. Nigel seemed shy, frightened even. Although he was excited and enthusiastic about the encounter, he was also very nervous and consequently found he was unable to get an erection. Fortunately Bob was an understanding lover and didn't make an issue of it. The sex was pleasant but clouded with an element of tension. Afterwards, when they were talking about other things, Bob found that he liked Nigel's outlook on life and his sense of humour. The two arranged to meet again, and once more they made love. This time Nigel was a little more relaxed, feeling reassured by Bob's patience and understanding.

**Nigel**: To be honest, the first time was a disaster. I felt as though I really wanted to have sex with Bob—he has a fabulous body—but I was so scared. I suppose I was frightened of making an idiot of myself. I'd only had one lover before and he was very much a wham-bam-thank-you-man sort of person. He just wanted an orgasm as soon as possible. Also I thought Bob would think my body wasn't very well-developed - I'm not very muscular. That first night with Bob I didn't have an orgasm, or even an erection if it comes to that, but it was still great.

**Bob**: I had asked Nigel to come back to my place because I liked his gentleness. He stood out from the disco crowd because he was so quiet and shy-looking. That appealed to me. He's also very pretty of course. I realised that he was nervous, he was actually trembling. I tried to be gentle with him, not doing anything startling or being rough. I know some men like aggressive sex, but Nigel wasn't ready yet. It was clear he was inexperienced.

**Nigel**: The second time we met—it was the following day—I couldn't wait to get my clothes off. I had been thinking about it all day and inventing all kinds of wonderful erotic things to do. But when the time came I was still shy, though not so much as the first time. I even managed to climax.

As they got to know each other better, they became more and more intense. Bob's feelings for Nigel grew and Nigel found in Bob the affectionate lover he had always hoped for. Their sex life began to flourish, and over the next few months it was almost a 'nightly orgy.' But there was no sense of routine about it; they were finding that sex was possible in all kinds of different places, not just bed. Sometimes the urgency they felt for each other would provoke sex in the bath, on the stairs, in the back of Bob's car and once even in the changing room of a department store. From a quiet start, Nigel had blossomed and Bob's patience had paid off. The lesson of their experience seems to be that if you like someone, find them attractive and feel that you can make something of your relationship—even though sex isn't great at first—it's often worth persevering until you trust each other.

The reverse can also be true of course, and sex that is fantastic, raunchy and earth-shaking at the beginning can fade very quickly when the novelty wears off and other areas of life intrude which aren't so passionate. Most people are sexually curious when they meet new partners and are happy to run the gamut of new experiences, but in established couples this curiosity can wane and routine sets in. Routine can quickly be followed by boredom, which in turn can lead to complete extinction of interest. The only way to stop this downward spiral is to be aware of it, not become complacent and resist routine. The answer is to be imaginative and refuse to the same thing in the same place every time. Vary the position and the environment.

Try this: make a date with your partner for a sexual tryst. Name the day, place, and time. Ensure that you don't have any other matters that need attending to and that the time will be entirely for sexual purposes. Make sure the place is not the same as usual (if you can possibly make an alternative to the bedroom, please do so. And if you can't, why not do it on the floor or up against the wall instead of in the bed?). Ensure that both of you are ready to try something completely different to your usual stuff, and then go ahead. If you need any equipment or peripherals (lube, condoms, toys, towels, paper) make sure they are to hand.

Try not to become one of those couples who, after a while in their relationship, say: "We only have sex on Sunday morning, and it's always the same." Do it standing up, sitting down or standing on your head, but do it differently from time to time.

## He Only Wants Sex and I Want Cuddles

Most gay men get a big thrill out of the physical closeness of other men. They like the smell of men, the feel of their bodies, the stubble on their chin, the strength of their arms, the hair on their chest and all the other things that comprise sexual interest. They like to be close in many ways, and kisses and cuddles are an important element of all this. Indeed, many gays have said that the biggest thrill they get from sex with other men is not so much genital stimulation (which is, nonetheless, important) but sleeping with their arms around each other, or cuddling together for hours on end or simply holding hands and watching TV.

Unfortunately, some men are so hung about their sexuality that they find kissing and cuddling generates feelings of discomfort so intense that expressing affection towards other men in this way becomes impossible; it is seen as a threat and a challenge to their masculinity. These men much prefer to have genital sex only, with minimum contact before and after. It is not so much that they don't crave affection in the same way that others do, it is just that expressing that tenderness is very difficult, because it compromises their image of themselves as 'normal'. It also

189

demands an element of communication which some men find extremely difficult to handle.

If you are in a relationship with such a man—or, indeed, if you yourself find kissing and cuddling or talking about sex uncomfortable—then you should be aware that your partner might feel deprived. Discuss it, and if your partner, or you, feel that more tactile affection is necessary, then see whether you can make some concessions. Simply bringing the problem out into the open is often enough. If partners are aware of the problem and are reassured that it is not a personal rejection of them, they might be able to live with it.

## Differing Needs, More Or Less

Another area of 'incompatibility' which people often cite as a problem is partners not having the same level of appetite for sex. One might want it every night, while the other would be happier if it were only once a week. What's the answer in such circumstances?

Bear in mind what we have discussed already about the 'stages' of a relationship, and how lovers can move from one stage to another ahead of their partner. Sexual activity diminishes as a relationship matures, but partners don't necessarily lose interest at the same rate. Just knowing this can often offer some kind of reassurance.

If, after honest consideration, you decide that the difference in your sexual needs is not a temporary situation (which can be brought on also by stress, overwork or other factors), then you could try to negotiate a compromise. Could the less sexually active partner bring himself to increase the ration to, say, three times a week? Would that satisfy the other? Is masturbation a satisfactory stop-gap or will the partner who wants more sex be allowed to find it outside the relationship? Negotiate carefully and don't be tempted to throw around accusations which might have devastating results ("You're undersexed / oversexed, you ought to get help."). If a partner is temporarily off sex because of outside pressures, then the other should try to be understanding and supportive. Lulls in your sexual life will be inevitable if you stay together over a long period - other factors are bound to intrude from time to time. Be patient with each other during such periods and they will right themselves.

If your partner is off sex for a while, try to understand why his libido has suddenly diminished. Is he working too hard? Has he suffered some stressful event in his life, like a bereavement or a demotion at work? If you can't find any reason which is immediately apparent, you may have to start looking at the very core of your relationship. Is everything working in other areas of your life together? Are there unresolved tensions between you? Far better to get to the root of these problems than to rush off to find sexual satisfaction elsewhere and end up putting even more pressure on the partnership. After all, it is perfectly possible to live without sex - many people do. You won't die from a quiet spell in your sex life.

Many gay relationships operate in comparative isolation and there is little opportunity to compare notes with other people in similar situations. Most gay couples are curious, nonetheless, about how other gay couples lead their lives. Academic researchers Peplau and Cochran surveyed 128 American gay men in relationships in 1976 to find out how often they had "had genital sex with each other over the past month". These are their findings which were published in *The Journal of Homosexuality:*

43% reported having sex less than twice a week.
27% said they had sex two or three times a week
30% said they had sex together more than three
times a week.

A British survey of gay men's sexual habits (Project Sigma) revealed that "the average gay man" wanks every other day, has sex with someone once a week (during which they wank, suck and body rub) and fucks every other week."

Naturally much will depend on what stage your relationship has reached. If it's early days then the frequency of sexual activity is likely to be higher than after five or six years. Other factors can also have an effect, and there is no such thing as 'the norm' in sexual desire. Whatever feels right for you is your own personal norm. These figures are shown just for interest.

## Safer Sex

Maybe your circumstances dictate that you must have safer sex with your partner (and it would be advisable to do so if there is any possibility that either of you has come into contact with HIV). It may be that one of you is HIV positive and the other negative or that you're both positive. Safer sex means, basically, that neither of you will allow the body fluids - semen, blood, mucous, vomit, piss, shit - of the other into his own body. This means no unprotected fucking or other kinds of penetrative sex that potentially allow fluids from one person to enter another's blood stream. "Protected" fucking means wearing a condom, which is better than nothing but doesn't carry any guarantees of safety. Condoms can break, come off or leak.

Injectors of illegal drugs, who have shared equipment, are also at risk from HIV infection, so ensure you know as much about your partner's history in that department as you can.

It may all seem terribly negative, but it needn't be - as Jeremy Laurence wrote in London's *Sunday Correspondent*:

> "There could be a different way of looking at Aids. It could provide an opportunity for reassessing our sexuality, its meaning and its pleasures. All we hear about is unsafe sex - as if we could ever be safe. Half its appeal lies in its risks, its excitements and its disappointments."

With this in mind, gay men have begun to redefine what exactly they think of as a "sexual encounter". They have begun to eroticise ever more parts of the body - perhaps using massage as the starting point for their conducted tour of every highway and byway of their partner's anatomy. They have explored fetishes: leather, denim, uniforms, working clothes. Some have embraced sado-masochism as a concept - emphasising the sexual power-broking inherent in domination and submission. This is often expressed in the inflicting of pain, although many experienced S & M practitioners are happiest with symbolic pain (and no blood-letting). Areas such as humiliation and bondage are being explored. Despite the political arguments against such activities (that S&M is really an expression of our self-loathing) people continue to experiment with them. Sexual desire is no great respecter of political correctness.

If we recognise the safer sex restrictions, the field is still wide open for a lot of variation. The more gay men think about it, the more ingenious they become in inventing ways to explore sex without penetration. Body rubbing, variations on a theme of masturbation, sex toys, pornography, oils and lubricants. Don't forget the famous - if somewhat esoteric - activity once described in a safer sex leaflet "dripping hot candle wax on your partner's skin". The possibilities are endless.

Neither should fantasy be underestimated as a means of enhancing sexual pleasure. Everyone has fantasies of some kind, and most of us become very adept at inventing erotic daydreams during our experiments with masturbation. You could exchange fantasies with your partner and then act them out (so long as nothing dangerous is involved and no-one is going to be coerced). Phil and Derek have used this technique when they have the time and the inclination. They will often work out elaborate "scenes" in which one of the plays the milkman or a policeman or a delivery boy and the other the householder who is summoned (scantily-clad, of course) from the bath.

**Phil**: I have this thing about policemen. I know it's a cliché, but I find the uniform and the hat and the big feet a real turn on. I think of *The Bill* as a blue movie in more ways than one. Anyway, we hired a policeman's uniform from the theatrical costumiers, and Derek dressed up in it. Then he came to the door and I invited him in. Derek then acts out this scene where the policeman has come to question me about some pornographic magazines and needs to take down my particulars. Then he gets rough and brutal and eventually rapes me, making me do all kinds of perverted things, all the time dressed in the uniform. Well, the tunic and helmet, anyway. I don't think I'd like it to happen in real life—in fact I know I wouldn't—but I'm aware it's only Derek and I know I'm safe and that means I

194

can concentrate on the erotic stuff and forget about the violence because it isn't real.

**Derek**: We know all the arguments about rape, and we think it's a horrible thing in real life. But no-one is hurt by our fantasy, and it gives us a great deal of pleasure. It lets me feel what it would be like to have power over someone. It encourages me to look at the dark side of my personality which, like most people, I subdue the rest of the time. I think we all have elements of selfish brutality in us and this particular little fantasy lets me express mine safely. I'd rather do it like this than truly overpower someone.

We've hired other costumes, too - sailor suits and ballet tights - and created fantasies around having it off with the window cleaner on his ladder and with this dishy Mormon who comes to the door trying to convert us. We don't do it very often because it takes such a long time to set up, but it's great fun. Although it sounds ludicrous when I say it out loud like this, it is actually quite sexy when you're playing it out and you let your imagination run riot. We can forget who we are and be different people doing different things.

The sexologists Masters and Johnson studied the sexual fantasy patterns of American homosexual men ("Homosexuality in Perspective" Little, Brown & Co, 1979) and found that the most popular images that gay men conjure up to enhance their sexual pleasure are:

**1.** Imagery of sexual anatomy - usually of penis or buttocks of someone other than their partner.

2. Forced sexual encounters. In nearly all circumstances the gay men fantasised themselves as the rapist.

3. Encounters with women - usually women from the gay man's past.

4. Having idyllic anonymous sex with an attractive stranger is a strong fantasy image. These daydreams usually revolve around a work colleague, entertainer or other person seen and fancied from a distance.

5. Group sex - the fantasiser often imagines himself observing an orgy rather than participating in it.

Anal intercourse remains a very powerful symbol for gay men; it seems to be the culmination of every erotic story and film you've ever seen. But, as many gay men are discovering, it is far from being essential for satisfactory sex. By all means use pornography as a source of ideas and enhancement, but always bear in mind that there are a lot of films in circulation which were made before the Aids crisis and whose actors do not practise safer sex. The fact they do it without a condom on the video or in the magazine you've bought doesn't mean that it is safe for you to be as irresponsible.

If you are both certain about your health status (either because your relationship started before 1975 and has always been sexually exclusive, because you've both had a series of antibody tests over a long period and found them to be negative or you were both virgins before you began) then you can freely explore most types of sex together. This is not to say that you have to do anything that you don't want to. The ability to say 'no' to a partner is one of the most powerful weapons in the safer sex armoury. If you don't want to have anal sex, then there is nothing mandatory about it —whatever impression you may have gained from videos or books. As Martin Allen wrote in *Boyz* magazine: "When I came out in the 70s, being fucked was standard, it was expected. And sometimes it bloody hurt. I was immensely relieved when it was no longer necessary to have anal sex; it was a real liberation."

So, whatever pressure you are under, always remember: you don't have to do anything you don't want to, whether it is anal sex, S&M, spanking or other activities. Keep your body under your own control, take responsibility for its safety.

Remember, too, there are many alternative orifices that can be employed - under the arm, between the thighs, between the buttocks (without penetrating and being careful not to allow semen to enter the anus) and so on. Don't forget lubrication to prevent friction burns.

The other things that can undermine resolve in safer sex practices are alcohol and drugs. If you get drunk or high, then inhibitions will be down and the temptation to go "all the way" might be strong, however aware you are of the dangers. Bear this in mind when you go to bed with your partner (or with your lovers away from your primary relationship). You might even decide beforehand on a signal you can use between you indicating that things are edging too far toward the unsafe. Perhaps a friendly slap on the bottom or a pull of the hair can be used to indicate that a change of direction is called for. This is less likely to break the erotic atmosphere than trying to explain to your partner in words that you are only prepared to play safely. Other threats to safer sex are over-excitement ("I can't wait until you find the condoms, it's now or never") or the idea that

197

condoms are unerotic ("It's like having a shower with a raincoat on, it deadens the senses") or inconvenient and difficult to manage ("Bugger this for a lark, let's just do it.").

Most gay men feel at some stage a strong urge to fuck or be fucked. For some it is the ultimate expression of intimacy and trust and becomes irresistible. In these circumstances, please make condoms part of your love play. Get into the routine of using them and don't make exceptions or become complacent. However much that you want to show your partner that you trust him, you can never be one hundred per cent sure that he is telling you the truth about his past or present sexual contacts. It might be that he is living in denial and simply not acknowledging the risks he might have taken.

Project Sigma found that men who entered committed relationships gradually abandoned safer sex practices with their regular partner.: "What seems to be happening is that within a relationship, the decision is being made to stop using a condom after a short while: the presumption being that the two can trust each other to have only safer sex outside the relationship because they love each other and somehow because of this they do not need to use condoms in the relationship. This misguided argument may have been reinforced by the government health campaigns which have encouraged sex within relationships, implying that the risk in these is less." The message is clear: being in love does not make either of you immune to HIV. Safer sex must continue until you are both certain (based on fact, not feeling) that it is safe to abandon it. The findings of this survey turn inside out the received wisdom that it is "safer" to stay in a relationship - it seems gay men take more precautions when they are having sex with casual partners than they do with their regular partner. Our desire to prove to our lover that we trust him maybe leading us into putting ourselves at risk of HIV infection.

Another significant finding of the survey was that of those who had never taken part in anal intercourse, none was HIV positive. This seems to reinforce the opinion that anal intercourse is by far the most effective means of spreading HIV among gay men. By abandoning anal intercourse, or ensuring that you always use a condom, you will dramatically reduce your chances of acquiring HIV.

## Condom Culture

We now have to think carefully about the mechanics of our sexual activities. Condoms should be part of our lives if we are sexually active. If you find it difficult to embarrassing to ask for them at a chemist, they can now be obtained from slot machines in public lavatories, many gay pubs and clubs, garages, record shops, pubs and barbers shops. Look out for the BSI Kitemark as this means that the condoms are able to pass the British Standards test for quality of manufacture. If we always use them, if they became part of our sexual routine, they will rapidly lose their unfamiliar feel.

Even if you aren't planning to fuck in the immediate future, buy a packet of condoms and play around with them just for the sake of removing the feeling of strangeness. During one of your wanking sessions try one on, following the instructions on the packet. Try it with different kinds of lubricants. You will find that if you use Vaseline or Nivea or butter or vegetable oil, the condom will disintegrate after a while. This is why it is important that you use a water-based lubricant such as KY. If you wank with the condom on you will find it is quite difficult to keep in place, and this will give you some idea of what might happen if you screw your partner while wearing a condom. If you treat it roughly it will tear. Practice is the answer, as with any other skill.

The Project Sigma findings showed that although users accepted that condoms provide protection against disease (and some found them erotic in their own right), there remained a significant resistance. They were felt by some to cause a loss of sensitivity and an interruption to sex. The physical attributes of the condom were disliked by 17 per cent and a few disliked their association with heterosexuals. About 18 per cent had experienced a condom tearing or slipping off.

## Negotiating Safer Sex - some tips

- When you are physically close to someone there might be too much excitement around to discuss things coolly. Don't be persuaded to do something you might regret later, so pick a moment beforehand when your head rules your feelings.

- If you are thinking of having penetrative sexual intercourse discuss using a condom with your partner. He may be plucking up the courage to mention the subject and the chances are that he will feel relieved rather than insulted. So don't beat about the bush - say something straightforward and simple like: 'Have you got a condom? If not, I have'. By playing safe you are teaming up together to protect each other.

- If you really can't discuss it, use a condom anyway or make a decision not to have high risk intercourse at all. Always remember to value your own judgements and try to feel able to say 'no' to something if it is outside the limits you have chosen.

- Take the initiative - carry your own condoms and don't rely on the other person. It's better for both of you to be prepared than neither.

- Remember to dispose of condoms safely by wrapping them in tissue and flushing them down the toilet.

## Safer Sex - the facts

- Anal sex carries the highest risk of transmitting HIV sexually with or without a condom (although, of course with is relatively safer). During anal intercourse, infected semen or blood can pass from one person to another through the lining of the anal passage and through tiny cuts and tears that can occur. The virus can also enter the penis through the opening at the tip or through scratches on the penis. Pulling out before ejaculation cannot be relied on to reduce the risk significantly.

- Fist-fucking, although extremely uncommon practice, is highly dangerous for both partners. It can tear the lining of the anal passage. Calving gloves, properly lubricated, reduce the risk of infection but do not eliminate it completely.

201

- There is no evidence that rimming (licking the anus) carries a risk of HIV transmission, but both partners can be at risk of other infections including hepatitis. This in turn *may* increase the risk of developing AIDS if you are already infected with HIV. Try using dental shields (or oral dams) which are rather like pieces of cling film. You put them over the anus and lick away. They act as a johnny for the tongue.

- Sharing sex toys like vibrators can also carry a risk as the virus can be passed on if you are sharing with someone who is infected, so keep to your own and make sure they can be easily distinguished.

- You cannot contract HIV by ordinary kissing and there is no conclusive evidence that it is transmitted by deep French kissing even though the virus has been found in small quantities in saliva. However, *theoretically* it is possible to be infected from deep kissing.

- Masturbation alone or with a partner is safe. You can ejaculate anywhere on his or your skin surface so long as semen which may contain the virus does not come into contact with open cuts or sores.

- Oral sex is one of the most popular gay activities. There is thought to be no risk if you are the person being sucked, but if you are doing the sucking and if you have cuts or sores in your mouth, there may be some risk. If you want him to ejaculate in your mouth it is safer if he wears a condom Oral sex, without getting pre-ejaculatory fluid (pre-cum) or semen in your mouth may be safe, however no-one is absolutely sure. Spermicides which coat some condoms can irritate the throat.

- Fingerfucking should be OK so long as you keep your nails short so as not to damage the delicate lining of the anus. It is best not to finger if you have open cuts or sores on your hands, even if covered with a plaster. You could try popping a condom over the digit or wearing surgical gloves.

- Massage is a safe, reliable and enjoyable activity. If you are using oils to enhance the experience make sure you don't let any oil-based lubricants get on to the condoms as they will perish the rubber.

- Rubbing your bodies together is perfectly safe. If you ejaculate it is still safe so long as semen which may contain the virus does not come into contact with any open cuts or sores you might have.

**Sexual Problems**

Happily, most researchers into sexuality have concluded that gay men experience fewer problems with their sexual functioning than do their heterosexual counterparts. This seems to be because straight men see sex as "goal-oriented" (the need to penetrate and ejaculate) whereas gay men are less focused and make their sexual encounters more wide-ranging and sensual experiences. Although anal intercourse is still seen as an important method of reaching orgasm, gay men tend to use other methods of stimulation more frequently to obtain their climax. Fellatio to orgasm seems to be more common among gay men and so does body rubbing. There seems to be less urgency these days for gay men to penetrate at all costs and, consequently, our sexual activities in general seem more imaginative.

Problems can still crop up, of course. Stresses which are unique to the gay experience (such as guilt about our sexuality) can wreak havoc. All the same, don't be too quick to claim you have 'sexual problems' when things go temporarily wrong. Defining what are often passing difficulties as 'problems' can give them a significance they don't deserve. As we've already said, sometimes a lessening of sexual interest might be connected with some other issue over which you partner has no control. Don't be in too much of a hurry to start fretting over the dips and troughs in the sexual landscape; there isn't a long-term relationship which hasn't experienced a sexual down-turn at some point. Most of the time it corrects itself and things get back on the rails. If it's a permanent turn of events then partners will adjust accordingly or make new arrangements.

If your partner suddenly finds difficulty in getting or maintaining an erection, there is certainly some reason for it - most of the time you don't have to look very far to see what it is. Difficulties in other areas of life are often the cause: stress, exhaustion, emotional upheaval, personal loss - all can bring on temporary problems. Some prescribed drugs can also affect the ability to get an erection as can over-indulgence in alcohol. Look at all these things and see if any of them are applicable and, if so, what can be done about them.

It may be that the erection failure is connected with the general state of the relationship. Most problems in bed can be related to problems out of it, so look at other areas of your life and see what is happening in them. Are there frictions which need to be resolved - hidden resentments that are making you feel less than loving? If you're too involved in the problem and find you can't 'see the wood for the trees', perhaps a counsellor could help you pinpoint it and sort it out?

The most common sexual difficulties experienced by men are premature and retarded ejaculation ('coming' to soon or not being able to come at all). These phenomena, too, are usually connected with something much deeper. The sufferer is often vulnerable and lacking in confidence. Premature ejaculation might show itself at the beginning of the relationship when excitement and apprehension mix in equal proportion. If someone suffers from a few episodes of premature or retarded ejaculation, it is likely that he will become anxious about it. The anxiety leads to and so a vicious circle of fear develops. In some instances, it really is just a matter of anxiety, and it calms down over a period of time. For some men, reaching orgasm quickly is just a function of their personality - just as speed of reaction differs in other areas of life, so it does with sex. Indeed, one sexologist found that on average, most men reach orgasm within two minutes of the beginning of direct genital stimulation.

However, if you consider premature ejaculation to be a problem in your relationship, there are simple and proven techniques for helping you last longer. Masters and Johnson, the American sex therapists invented the "squeeze technique" which is suitable for self-application. I explain this in more detail in my book *How to be a Happy Homosexual* (GMP Publishers). Another excellent and reassuring book is Bernie Zilbergeld's *Men and Sex* (published by HarperCollins). Although written from the viewpoint of a heterosexual man, it includes much information which gay men will find pertinent.

Sexual difficulties are always better tackled with the help of a loving and patient partner and, occasionally, with the help of a qualified sex therapist.

## One Man's Kinkiness...

...is another man's pleasure. The British popular press is very fond of writing about 'kinky' sex, which they seem to define as anything other than the missionary position as practised by married couples. Agony columns in straight newspapers and magazines reveal that many heterosexuals are tormented if they have the urge to have what they consider "perverted" sex (oral sex seems often to fall into this category as does cross-dressing and taking erotic Polaroids of each other). Gay men suffer less from these inhibitions and are mostly happy to try out new ideas. What some straight people consider to be sexually beyond the pale are the things that gay men enjoy most as a matter of course. So long as any potential risks are recognised (anything involving unprotected penetration, asphyxiation or bondage, for instance) and there is no element of coercion there need be few limits.

No-one would deny that the sexual urge is overwhelmingly powerful at times. It can motivate us to great heights of happiness and propel us to the depths of despair. Perhaps the desire for money is the only other motive that can cause people to take such extraordinary risks. I think there are few other activities that would impel normally timid people to jeopardise their safety and reputation as sex does. Ordinarily respectable and law-abiding citizens will put themselves at risk of arrest and public humiliation in order to go cottaging; men who in other circumstances are extremely prudent and cautious about their personal safety will happily take home complete strangers and thus put themselves on the line. Such is the strength of the sexual drive and the wonderful and frightening madness it can inspire.

## Communication

Perhaps the greatest sexual problem is poor communication. The whole relationship may suffer from this failing. Your partner is not psychic and you cannot expect him to know if you don't tell him what you want, how you feel and whether he is doing the right thing.

Breaking down communication barriers generally can be extremely difficult. Not only do we sometimes fail to tell our partner what we want or what we expect, we actually give completely the opposite message to the one we intended. Or we make things so obscure and confused that no-one really knows what is going on. Directness and honesty are the only ways around this.

If you want to talk about your sex life (particularly aspects of it which you might think are unsatisfactory or sensitive in some other way) set things up carefully in advance. Agree between you before you begin that the aim of your discussion is to improve your sex life. Both partners should be clear that they are not being attacked and need not, therefore, be defensive. It is this very reaction which stands in the way of our clearing up the difficulties which dog our lives together. Give each other the reassurance you need.

Tread carefully and be as diplomatic as you can - without sacrificing truth and directness. People who aren't used to talking openly about their feelings might not take kindly to being told—however constructively—that their sexual technique could do with some brushing up. Read again the techniques of negotiation, especially about owning your own feelings. Use sentences that begin with "I feel" rather than ones that begin "You ought to..."

## The Universal Hand Job

Many gay men continue to masturbate quite frequently even when they have a regular and satisfying partner. Research has shown that masturbatory life is likely to continue right through the relationship, however intensely sexual that relationship might be. Some men do it because their partner doesn't want as much sex as they do, some do it to relieve stress and others do it simply because they like the variation.

However much we love our partner, there are times when it's comforting to be completely alone with our sexual thoughts and feelings. We are all entitled to a bit privacy - even from our beloved. Be assured that most couples have separate masturbatory lives and it doesn't reflect at all on the quality of their life together.

## Reunions Need Time

If partners has been separated for some time—in some instances for only a few days—they might find a few difficulties in becoming a smooth-running couple again. However glad you are to see your partner returning home after an absence, you might also feel a vague sort of resentment. Perhaps you have prepared a lovely reunion surprise, only to find that within an hour of his coming into the house you are fighting like cat and dog over some trivial incident.

It may be that you've spent the preceding days, weeks or months psyching yourself up to being alone or that you've spent time while you were apart thinking about some aspects of the relationship which has irritated you. You might have felt lonely not having him around the house as usual, but you will also have adjusted to the routine of not having him there. The readjustment takes a little time. It is a common phenomenon and it quickly wears off as you get used to each other again.

Longer periods apart, perhaps because of work commitments (you decided not to go to Tahiti with him), need careful management. In these circumstances you should discuss your attitude to monogamy again - can you both manage for all that time without seeing someone else, even if only for sex? Would you prefer to know that you lover is finding comfort elsewhere or would you prefer to remain in blissful ignorance? How would you cope with any anxiety which might arise because of jealousy? Confront the problems before they arise - don't just wait for them to appear in a cloud of bitterness.

### Life without Sex

Many gay couples who have been together over a period of decades have told how their sexual life has gradually petered out. For the majority of them this is not the disaster it might sound. While their sexual activity diminished, their emotional attachment to each other grew ever stronger.

Some of them reported that they looked elsewhere for sexual contacts, but did not regard these as a threat to the primary relationship.

One couple I met has even decided to have a celibate relationship. This might seem a contradiction in terms, but their partnership is as strong and committed as any of the others I have seen, even though no sexual activity is involved. The couple were affectionate, loving and each considered the other the most important person in his life. They were unusual but they had made it work, and this indicates once again that we all have the capacity to make our lives fit into our own game-plans rather than somebody else's. We should not allow other people's expectations about what us "right", "correct" or "the only proper way", to coerce us into living in ways that are unsuitable for us.

## Ejaculation Isn't Always Essential

Perhaps the most liberating piece of information that can be given to couples who are unsure whether they are behaving "correctly" in their sexual life is that you don't have to shoot a load in order to have a satisfactory sexual experience. This will sound strange to men who have been raised to believe that the orgasm was the sole purpose of sex and that if you don't ejaculate you haven't really had sex. The number of times that men have failed to ejaculate, even after a lot of stimulation, and then considered that there was something wrong with them is tragic. Sometimes the body just will not co-operate and however hard you try, the ejaculation just will not come. It doesn't matter. So long as you've enjoyed your encounter in other ways, the orgasm is just a bonus at the end.

Sometimes people just want to have a naked cuddle, or a little bit of slap and tickle, without taking it the whole way—perhaps because they're too tired for an elaborate sexual experience—but still want to express closeness with their partner. Most gay couples come to an agreement about this and know when it is OK to say: "Do you mind if I go to sleep now?" An ejaculation is not the inevitable consequence of every hard-on you get. If you cling to the notion that sex is always and inevitably about coming, do yourself a favour and think again. Orgasms are great, but they aren't essential every time.

## Quickies Have Their Place

Most of us feel pressured at times - we have to get up early for work, we have to rush from one appointment to the another, the house needs cleaning, the shopping needs doing, the ironing is piling up. Sometimes it feels that there aren't enough hours in the day to keep our complicated lives running. In the midst of all this frantic activity sex can slide pretty far down the scale of priorities. You just don't seem to have the time or the energy.

It's in busy periods like this that quickies come into their own. So long as you both know that it's just to release the pressure, a rapid sexual episode can be most pleasing and convenient. For instance, first thing in the morning you're feeling sexy - you've woken up with a throbbing hard on and you're hot to trot. The trouble is it's half past seven and you've got to be at your desk in an hour. Will your partner mind if it's just wham-bam-thank-you-Sam for now? Probably not. So a quickie can reassure him that you're still interested in sex, even though your busy schedule doesn't allow for an elaborate swinging from the chandeliers session just at the moment.

## To Summarise:

1. Negotiate your own sex life - don't worry what other people consider to be normal, do it your own way.

2. Stick to safer sex unless you are both absolutely certain about your antibody status. Being in love is no protection from Aids.

3. Look for alternatives to anal intercourse. If you're determined to fuck ALWAYS use a condom.

4. Don't be too quick to claim you have a sexual problem. Often they work themselves out given time. Anxiety and tension can be the cause, and if problems persist, seek expert advice.

5. Don't fall into a rut. Make a conscious effort to vary your activities. Make a date with your partner for a time a place and a good time.

6. Don't use sex as a means of manipulating your partner, it's too precious an asset to use in this way.

7. Sexual secrets can cause problems in your sex life. Try to find a way of sharing your secret desires with your partner. Make a pact not to be judgmental when you share your fantasies.

8. Don't panic when sex becomes less frequent of when there are temporary lulls in your sex life - it happens to everybody.

9. You don't have to have an orgasm every time you have sex.

10. Don't despise quickies - they can fulfil a useful purpose when time is short but your libido is reminding you that it's still there.

# Chapter Ten:

# The end of the road

All good things must come to an end and that includes relationships. The end might be bitter, it might be tragic, it might simply be a relief. But endings are as important as beginnings and if you think carefully about your options, you can save yourself much pain and anguish.

## Breaking Up Is Hard To Do...

...or so go the words of the song. In some cases splitting up is the best thing that could happen to a relationship which has become sour or moribund. You will know if you are in such a partnership - you'll feel trapped, manipulated, abused or simply bored. If the only true happiness you get is when you are away from your partner, then a permanent break might be the best for both of you.

But wait - don't be too hasty in branding your relationship a failure. Sometimes all that is needed is better communication, better negotiating skills, more acceptance of change and a tad more give and take. Even if your home seems like a battleground, where every issue becomes an argument or fight, there may still be hope for you. Read again the chapters on Ground Rules and Relationship Skills and see if you can't make a new start utilising the suggestions made there. Maybe it's too soon for you to be singing what the American lesbian writer Betty Berzon called the Gay National Anthem, the refrain of which goes: "This isn't working out, maybe we should split. It isn't like it used to be, let's call it a day."

The reason most couples get into a pattern of argument, resentment and abuse is because their relationship lacks one or more of the three cornerstones we talked about before: trust, acceptance and respect. If you spend your time together in an orgy of bitterness and recrimination, just ask yourself whether the three elements are truly part of your love. If they aren't—and even if one of them is missing it will have a devastating effect—then think of ways you can introduce them. This means both of you, of course: the relationship is beyond repair if either partner is unwilling to work hard for its survival. Only you can judge whether the effort would be justified. And before you dismiss this suggestion, just remember that if you aren't prepared to acknowledge the necessity of the cornerstones in your present relationship, it's unlikely that you'll take them with you into the next and so the pattern will repeat itself. Rather than give up immediately, why not try to revive your existing partnership with the hard work it needs?

Once you have decided to have another go, remember the rules of negotiation and apply them. Only if you respect each other will you be able to go into negotiations with the determination that both of you will win something. Only if you are prepared to break the old patterns of power play and manipulation will you both feel that your partnership gives you enough satisfaction to justify its continuation. You can choose to make the relationship one between two mature, consenting adults or you can continue to behave like fractious children, selfishly refusing to see each other's point of view. Read this book again and ask yourself whether ditching your present combative or non-communicative system of functioning and replacing it with what is recommended here will give you a better chance of success.

To change behaviour patterns is notoriously difficult, but it isn't impossible. We've all met people who've managed to give up smoking, sometimes thirty or forty a day, even though they seemed hopelessly addicted. We've seen the before and after pictures of champion slimmers who have changed their ingrained eating habits in order to lose weight. Don't underestimate the difficulty of these achievements, but also don't imagine that you couldn't perform a similar transformation of destructive behaviours within your relationship.

## Letting Go

But suppose it really is over. You feel deep in your heart that your life is diminished rather than enhanced by your partner. How can you let go? Are you staying in a dead relationship because you are afraid of the consequences of leaving? There is no doubt that starting again (particularly if your partnership is of long standing) will be difficult in the extreme. There will be inevitable periods of unhappiness and confusion which might cause you to lose confidence for a while and doubt your ability ever to be able to love again. Holding on to a relationship which brings misery is common, because at least it is misery that you know; fear of the unknown seems even worse. In gay couples there might be other reasons for sticking around even though there doesn't seem much to be sticking around for. Lack of confidence, fear that there won't be another opportunity for a relationship, the sheer terror of being alone. There might also be the financial considerations. If one partner has come to depend on the other for a home, for instance, moving out will be more than just a matter of emotional considerations.

But think about it for a moment; what is the worst that can happen if you pack up and move out of a dead relationship? You might be lonely for a while, but you're probably feeling lonely anyway, even within the relationship. You might feel like a failure and have doubts about your capacity to love or be loved. This is a temporary frame of mind and you must constantly remind yourself of that. You might think that after all these years, you won't be able to cope alone. You've been part of a twosome for so long now that you can't imagine what it would be like having to go out into the big, wide, unsympathetic world as a solo act. It might be difficult, but it won't be impossible. Your standard of living may drop for a while, but you'll adjust. And don't forget, you managed somehow before you met your partner. It's unlikely that you can honestly say that your life was impossible or worthless before he came along. Remember the good times you enjoyed as a single person. You never know, you might find your return to a solo life has considerable benefits, if you seek them out.

## The Aftermath

There is no getting away from the fact, though, that your parting will be followed by a period of grieving and loss. You probably invested a great deal of emotional energy in

the relationship, had high hopes for its future and now here
it is in ruins at your feet. Don't chide yourself too bitterly. I
have already encouraged you to accept imperfections in
your partner, and now I am asking you to recognise that
you, too, are imperfect. You may have made a mistake
(although, often even at this point, you may be able to say
you were enriched by it) but it isn't the end of the world.
You're entitled to make mistakes - we all are - and you're
entitled to admit them and forgive yourself. Maybe you
entered your relationship knowing that your partner had big
problems, and maybe you misjudged your ability to deal
with them. Maybe you simply didn't understand what was
needed to make a relationship work and you feel you drove
your partner away. Learn from these mistakes, forgive
yourself, try to remember some positive aspects of the
relationship and then move on.

If the parting was quiet, negotiated and mutually agreed,
the pain is likely to be less intense and last for a shorter
time. You will have suffered much of the grieving process
already If the bust-up was volcanic, an explosion of
recrimination and accusation, then the pain may be acute
and long-lasting. Not many relationships end by civilised
mutual agreement, unfortunately (although my observations
indicate that more end this way in the gay world than
straight). Often one partner makes the decision to leave. In
that case it is the one who leaves rather than the one who is
left who, psychologically, has the better part of the deal (if
there can be a better part of a broken relationship). The
partner who has been left will probably feel the loss of
confidence more acutely, particularly if his lover has left
him for someone else. If you find yourself in this unhappy
position, try to accept that because your partner has gone on
to pastures new, it doesn't invalidate you as a person. Your

partner has the same right as you have to get from a relationship those things which will enrich his life. Just because you weren't the person to provide his particular cocktail of virtues doesn't mean that you are utterly worthless. Maybe he needed someone who shared his religious commitment or his sporting aspirations or who was interested in philosophy. Maybe you didn't fulfil those needs. That doesn't make you bad or inferior, it simply doesn't make you the right person for him.

When you've recovered a little, you will come to realise that you, like everyone else, have a right to say: "I have only one life and I want to live it with the person who brings me most happiness." (or even alone). When you've accepted this, you'll probably find it within yourself to forgive your ex-lover, although it may take some time and a lot of courage. It's a good step towards regaining your own sense of self-worth. One day you might find yourself with the boot on the other foot. If you have to leave a lover because your own particular happiness lies elsewhere, then you should forgive yourself and do what is necessary.

This is a difficult concept to grasp when you feel you have been jilted. A little self-pity is permitted in those circumstances, but keep it under control. Nobody likes the maudlin sort of person who cries for ever over the way life has treated him - and it won't do anything to speed your recovery, either. Thinking positively about yourself and your future is impossible if you are wallowing in mawkishness.

When you've parted the pain may be so intense that you will thrash about looking for ways to relieve it; unfortunately there are no emotional aspirins to combat this kind of agony. But beware, lurking round the corner are a number of apparent escape-routes: drinking might bring temporary relief, but you will eventually have to sober up and face the music; tranquillisers or other drugs might obliterate the crisis temporarily, but they have their own dangers, and they don't solve the problem. When you emerge from the drug-induced haze, your loneliness is still there and your pain has not gone away.

Tempting as these palliatives might be, resist them - far from solving your difficulties they often make them worse by introducing the complication of addiction.

It could well be that your parting has been civilised and you pledged to remain friends. But don't expect too much too soon from such a promise. You can't expect to see your lover, perhaps with his new partner, two days after you've moved out and feel nothing but unalloyed pleasure. A thousand and one issues may need sorting out before you can regard him as a 'proper' friend. It may be that your parting was drawn out over a long period, in which case you might have resolved many of the more emotionally draining issues before you moved out. Maybe you have no regrets whatever about splitting, and are rapturous at being free. This won't be true for most people, who will suffer a period of sleeplessness, self-blame, other-blame and depression. This is natural. Don't be too quick to label yourself "neurotic" because you cry all night and can't eat your meals for a week. If he has left you for another partner there might also be feelings of jealousy that are all the more tormenting because there seems nothing you can do to relieve them. You suffer agony because you are alone and they have each other.

## Finding Support

When gay relationships end, it can be a trauma of the first order. It could also be difficult to find the support that is needed to get you through the crisis. If the relationship has been conducted in the closet, then the lovers will probably have to manage on their own. This is particularly cruel and difficult - being deeply unhappy and not being able to discuss it with anyone is torment of the highest order. The answer is in your own hands: read again the chapter on Other People's Approval. Even those who are out of the closet might have difficulty finding sympathy among their straight friends and family. Some straight people are unable to accept that gay relationships are as deep and serious as their own: they may shake their head, smile knowingly and repeat the I-told-you-so propaganda which says gay relationships don't last. However tempting it might be, don't fall for it. Instead, seek help and reassurance in the gay community. Bend the ears of friends interminably about your misery (explaining that you are about to bore them into the ground, and promising that one day you'll return the favour if they need it). And when your friends grow weary of listening to you, then turn to the gay helplines or befriending agencies who will listen as long as you like (remember that Lesbian and Gay Switchboard in London operates twenty-four hours a day, so you can talk yourself hoarse during a crisis). This constant talking about the consequences of your break up will act as a catharsis, it will help you empty out the misery, discharge it into the ether.

## On The Rebound

Soon after the shock and dismay of seeing a primary relationship end, there may be a severe loss of confidence. You will begin to ask yourself why it happened, and if your partner has found someone else there may be feelings of profound jealousy. The loss of confidence can have many effects - one of which is bad decision-making. If you are seeking to have your esteem bolstered, you may feel desperately that you need 'someone else' immediately. This might be simply to reassure yourself that you're still attractive enough to get someone, it might be a means of trying to escape the pain and loneliness you feel. Whatever the reason, make sure you realise what is happening. If you are depressed and in emotional turmoil you might think that starting a new relationship immediately will be the perfect answer. You imagine that you can recapture all the good things that your last relationship gave you - and perhaps even better it. But this is not necessarily a good move. Are you going into this new partnership simply as a means of recapturing the old one? The rebound effect is well known and yet almost everyone who is upset by the failure of a relationship is tempted to fall into the trap. It seems such a simple answer to all those problems.

Most couples see what is happening before they go too far. The new partner comes to realise that he has not been chosen on his own merits, but as a replacement or to soothe your loneliness. It may be that the jilted lover realises that he is importing all the unresolved problems into his new relationship. In other cases, both may recognise the unfairness of such an arrangement. If both partners realise what is going on, and take their time, such partnerships may eventually work on their own terms. However, it takes patience, goodwill and understanding for a new partner to wait until his lover has let go of his old relationship.

It may take several attempts before you feel you've found the relationship that will really work. The truth is that some relationships in your life are more important than others, and sometimes it takes a while before it is clear whether a particular relationship is going to pay off. It follows that not all partings will be as traumatic as the ones described here, but each one will generate some emotion (even if it is only a sigh of relief) and each will have taught you something about yourself and other people. Use the knowledge you have gained to help you in future relationships.

Another phenomenon which we have already discussed occurs with gay men who have never really accepted their sexuality as valuable is the blame-homosexuality-syndrome. It goes something like this: "I'm gay and, as everyone knows, gay relationships don't last. Therefore all my relationships are unsatisfactory. Gay men are so fickle, they don't want commitment, they just want one night stands. It would be different if I were normal, straights don't treat each other like this."

What this really means is: "I don't like being gay and, underneath it all, I don't really believe that gay relationships have any value. Therefore I set myself up for failure by seeking out people who aren't ready to settle down or people who are playing the field or people who have big emotional problems. When I try to make relationships with them I am always disappointed and I blame the failure on the fact that I'm gay."

The answer here is to (a) start to look at your sexuality more positively and (b) learn how to make more realistic assessments about the intentions of people you meet. If it's clear that your contact is simply asking for an evening of sex, then you must either accept it or reject it on those terms. It's no use trying to force commitment on people who don't want it—that's inviting disappointment. A relationship will only work if both partners are rooting for it, and that applies equally to homosexuals and heterosexuals.

## 'Til Death Us Do Part

Only in rare circumstances do loving partners die together; most of the time one will be bereaved and left to pick up the pieces of a shattered life. Aids has brought death to the forefront of many gay lives; more gay men will die before their time as the crisis deepens. More relationships will end before the partners have had an opportunity to fully explore their lives together.

How do you cope with the loss of someone you have come to love more than anyone else in the world? How do you carry on when the partnership you treasured so deeply is shattered so finally? And what if a partner becomes ill with HIV disease - will you be able to cope with the consequences of this experience?

One man who has been through this trauma, and who has written about it memorably, is Bruce Hugman. Bruce has written movingly in *Gay Times* of the last months of his relationship with his lover, Roy. He has given me permission to reproduce some of that story here in the hope that it will inspiration to others who find themselves in similar circumstances. The discovery that one partner is HIV positive is a nightmare that many of us would prefer not to contemplate, but for an increasing number of gay couples, the nightmare is becoming reality. That is why we must learn from each other's hard-won experience. Here is how Bruce and Roy coped with the discovery of Roy's positive status:

"Over last Christmas and the New Year his persistent debility, night sweats and loss of appetite made him suspect that something serious was wrong. The several weeks of painful sinus infection and dry convulsive coughing took him eventually to the doctor, fearing the worst. But that premonition did nothing to soften the steely impact of the positive result.

That day, I arrived home late in the evening (oh god, to be absent at such a time!) - to find him sitting pale, bolt upright in bed with the news instantly, cataclysmically on his lips. Stunned by turns we talked mechanically, or wept in each other's arms - faced suddenly, unambiguously with the possible end of all we had built together, all we had planned for the future, the final act of a life that had hardly begun. That night there were moments of rage and grief, of beating the bedclothes with despair and frustration, but nothing to the climax of reaction ahead.

The next day (a Friday) we spent together at home, intensely, closely, talking—amongst much else—with uncanny coolness about very practical matters—wills, life assurance, maintaining our income, paying the mortgage— talking as if he were about to die—for that it is how it felt to him: it seemed as if the news had itself not only given him the disease, but also pronounced a sentence of imminent death.

In the height of the early shock, we agreed to tell no-one else. This fearful, depressed reaction rapidly gave way, as we thought of our kindly, supportive friends, to a determination to tell most of them: secrecy would only intensify our sadness and cut us off from those very resources that would provide comfort and hope.

It was the sense of injustice which, I think, he felt most - we had both for so many years been careful, responsible. It may have happened before we knew there were risks to take or choices to be made - eight, ten years ago: oh, the unfairness of it! 'Why me? Why me?'

The following evening (Saturday) he was booked to go out with two dear friends of ours (we have always enjoyed some social life independently of each other) while I remained at home.

Very late, the three of them returned, our friends leading him pale, unsteady, drunk beyond measure from the taxi. He slumped on the stairs, weeping raspingly, while they went into the front room in floods of choking tears. Evidently he had told them. I closed the door and stayed on the stairs with him. He was desperate, furious, grief-stricken, violently, helplessly angry. 'Bastard life! Bastard life!' he hissed again and again through his sobbing.

Slowly, the peak of anger passed. We returned to the room. Our friends' grief at the thought of losing someone they loved so much—and others who might fall victim too—was violent, and they cried and cried, hurt and fearful, as we sat successively in each other's arms till early morning - tear ducts aching and wide open.

It was a time of the most extravagant grief I have ever come close to - dear people overcome, overtaken, utterly overpowered by one commanding emotion. I alone remained dry-eyed and unaccountably calm.

He and I woke together on Sunday strangely relaxed and cleansed - the depths seemed to have been plumbed and were now passed. The climax—the nadir—was now over.

So we told many—most—of our friends during the following days and weeks. It prompted such an outpouring of love and support and concern that it was exhilarating and beautiful. It was as if knowledge of death allowed hearts to be opened in a way sometimes only apparent at funerals - when the frank declaration of love and appreciation is tragically too late to enrich the life of the loved one.

There is no cynicism in this - for even doing our best, most of us have learnt only too late that we could, should have done better - should not have wasted those precious times when love was felt but not shown.

If our friends comfort and sustain us, there is also much else that gives us strength: we feel great pride and pleasure in our gay and lesbian brothers and sisters and in our community, especially now, knowing at first hand at a time of need their practical, effective and generous responses to the reality of the virus and the disease; pride that 'our' people and their many friends have confronted the nightmare with imagination, responsibility and maturity.

Knowledge of death concentrates the mind and the affections. We do not feel that we have wasted our nearly seven years together - we have had a full, varied and modestly adventurous life; we have not seriously abused or neglected each other; we have had a good time in two excellent homes with many much-loved friends.

Now we know all that could end soon, we are changing our priorities to some extent: it is less relevant to save for the future now - we should spend and enjoy. We should do some of the things we have always wanted to do. We should make the most of the time, the people, the opportunities. We should do everything we can to stay in our home—if he must be ill, let it be here—and so I must earn to compensate for the possible loss of his wages. We must sort out the practical and financial affairs.

So - we have flown Concorde (ninety minutes of supersonic luxury, champagne all the way); next we may blow our savings on the Orient Express or in a flight round the world; we are spending our time with our friends; we are going to more concerts and plays; we are taking more quiet time together; I have left a modest, stable job and set up my own business; we have had serious sessions with our solicitors and executors. Our house is in material order; we are not in retreat.

He still cries himself to sleep from time to time, fearful for the future; is still occasionally angry and resentful; is often weary. I sometimes wake up with tears in my eyes and an ache in my throat, or find myself about to weep on the street or the train. If I let myself, I fear for the future horribly; his suffering, my inadequacy, the end, whenever, to come.

In the early days of knowing he was HIV+ we found it worrying and difficult to be out of each other's company for any length of time. For him it was, I think, his shocked sense of sudden weakness and vulnerability - alone, he felt at risk from his demon body, and frail in a world that had suddenly delivered such a hostile blow to his hopes. For us both it was a compelling need simply to be together, while my early and continuing fear was that something dramatic might happen when I was away from him.

I have found it very difficult, without a sense of unreasonable guilt, to continue meeting the demands of my business, and allow myself to become absorbed in the outside world and its concerns. It's a particularly painful process because I miss his best hours of the day: he's asleep (or at least sleepy) when I leave in the morning, and weary by the time I return in the evening. Yet it obviously has to be done if we are to stay here, comfortably in our home, when he can no longer earn.

After about eight weeks or so we had just about come to some kind of terms with HIV on a day to day basis, though he was not in good health and we feared there was definitely something wrong. He continued to work through that time, taking his lunch hours for clinic visits, which we made together.

I arrived home one afternoon to find him packing a suitcase: he was to be admitted to hospital for investigation of a patch on his lung which had shown up on X-ray.

It was devastating news. In dealing originally with the reality of the positive test, one of our strategies had been to reflect that at least the result did not make him ill, and that it could be a long time before illness emerged. That was swept away - he now had PCP, one of the most typical 'opportunistic' infections of a damaged immune system, and we had to accept that he was more vulnerable than we had hoped.

In the early days, amidst the grief and drama, we were also very business-like in attending to practical affairs, and we have since been grateful for that foresight.

After a couple of years of living together, we had made wills, appointing each other as executors along with his brother-in-law and my brother, and making each other principal beneficiaries of our estates.

Knowing, however, that our relationship had no status in law, and that meddling bureaucrats or unsympathetic medical authorities could stand between us or seek to discount our wishes (all facts and possibilities which make us angry and indignant) we wanted, in view of the new situation, to strengthen our position.

## Making Gay Relationships Work

We arranged a meeting with our solicitors and executors. First, we signed slightly revised wills. Second, we read out, and then had signed and witnessed, a statement declaring our absolute wishes with regard to our rights over each other. This says, essentially, that all persons and authorities are to regard us as nearest next of kin of the other with regard to all practical and financial matters, with regard to hospital visiting and access to medical information, and with regard to funeral arrangements. We also appended a paragraph from the 'Living Will' of the Voluntary Euthanasia Society which asks that life should not be artificially or painfully prolonged.

This declaration probably has no ultimate legal status, but it at least means that our solicitors and families are in no doubt at all about, and have formally (and willingly) consented to our wishes.

Finally, we both signed 'Powers of Enduring Attorney' for each other. This does have full legal status, and is enforceable in the courts. On formal registration it empowers each of us to act in law *as if he were the other person* - to sign cheques, make contracts, dispose of property and so on. Within the current state of our unhelpful legal system it is the nearest a gay couple can approach to achieving the rights and benefits of marriage. It is the most absolute act of mutual commitment in legal terms.

To those who have not thought deeply about such matters, or who have not experienced the sheer indifference—brutality even—of families and people in positions of authority in the face of a gay partner or bereaved lover, all this may seem completely over the top. It is not: when it comes to the crunch our world can still be mean, hostile and cruel. The risks are too great to be left to chance.

So, when he was admitted to hospital, it was one less anxiety to know that we'd been through all the formalities - at the worst I could show an obstructive sister the Power of Attorney and threaten to go to court."

*For two years, Bruce and Roy lived with the knowledge of possible premature death, and with the gradual disintegration of Roy's health. Bruce now describes what happened subsequently:*

"He died at home in his sleep, just after five in the morning. His breathing slowed, thinned and evaporated effortlessly. I held his hand and said good-bye. I did not cry then.

The previous ten days had been rough for both of us; for him as he became increasingly helpless - recently blind, progressively debilitated, unable to swallow more than a few drops of liquid at a time, subject to the tyranny of the congested chest, nauseous stomach, and unpredictable bowels; for me, working and nursing, beyond all the boundaries of physical and emotional resources I had ever crossed before.

Yet though he suffered so much, it was only at some point on the last day that the final hair's breadth of quality of life disappeared for him - the point at which I knew, and I'm sure he knew that there could be nothing more to take pleasure in. Only then was he ready, and I was willing, at last to let go.

What mattered for both of us was quality of life, not quantity. His choice for a shorter and better life was uncompromising and we were fortunate in having a medical

231

team who understood such things and offered that choice. We learnt that quality of life is not necessarily some grand and sumptuous state, and absolutely not about hankering for some vision of what might have been: it is about achieving the best that is possible in the present moment. While he was active and relatively well, quality was achieved by exploiting all our available resources—physical, emotional, financial—and doing everything that we could.

As he became weaker, house bound and eventually bed-ridden, so the scope of quality narrowed, and we adjusted progressively to what was possible, but its richness did not diminish.

What he was able to do, with astonishingly courageous realism, was to reconcile himself to each loss of strength, faculty, opportunity to live fully within the boundaries of what was possible within the present. Two examples illustrate this extraordinary adaptability - the wisdom of which I could only follow with humility.

For the last six months he was—as we both wished—at home. In the early days he would be up and about for a few hours each day while I was at work and then have an afternoon snooze. He got up when I came in, we ate together and spent the evening talking together with friends, on the phone or watching TV or videos. Gradually he spent more and more time in bed during the day, getting up only after I'd been in for an hour or two, and spending just a couple of hours dozing on my lap on the sofa before going back to bed. They were hours of quiet, undemanding, lovely intimacy.

Exploring his perception of the quality of his life, the consultant asked him if his day with this couple of good hours was good enough. In a powerful phrase—all the more so for being quite untypical in its language—he said, 'It's

232

sufficient'. And he continued to enjoy those couple of hours until he could no longer haul himself up and down the stairs, when the criteria for quality had to be redefined once again.

The other indication of his capacity to hold precious the moment was much later when he was blind and bedridden, and when the arena of quality was becoming relatively microscopic. He was eating nothing—and drinking very little—that little dripped into his mouth from a syringe. On two nights he woke up wanting a drink. The first time he asked for milk. I brought him half a pint straight from the fridge, and he insisted on sitting up on the edge of the bed. He drank half at one go and said, 'That is so beautiful.'

On the second occasion, after reviewing the range of drinks in the house, he said he'd like an ice cream soda, with ice cream in it. He had one, adored it, and promptly asked for another - the evident immediate pleasure being enriched by childhood memories of similar, exceptional indulgence.

In the midst of raging illness, debility, helplessness, such moments have a kind of glory about them - in spite of everything, he was able to give himself over to intense pleasure. There was, then, a hair's breadth of quality, which was, at the time, for him, no less full and real than drinking champagne on the Orient Express had been the previous year. He could release the Orient Express as a possibility and savour the next focus of quality though it was on a ever-diminishing scale. Only when there was nothing left on the scale did he choose to die.

Quality was not simply delicious drinks in the middle of the night. His ability to adapt to shrinking horizons stemmed from his own heroic strength, but also from much else which fed that strength and allowed it to flourish.

One element was certainly being at home - the home we had created together, on which he had lavished such care, in which we had had such happy times together and with friends. Wonderful though the loving care had been on the ward, there is something enervating and debilitating about being in hospital. However generous the regime, you are not in charge, cannot call the tune, are not on your own territory. We were both clear that we wanted him to be cared for at home - and he wanted, as he said, to die on our sofa with his head in my lap.

That the ward staff and the community care team unreservedly understood and accepted this choice of ours put us back in charge and left us to live freely according to our own rhythms.

We were given a degree of control, too, in full participation in planning the immensely complex, constantly changing medical and drugs regime. Opting for quality led to the decision, for example, to start on steroids, with all the possible–but to us both, acceptable–risks. And similarly, constantly in every respect the costs and benefits of one course of action or another were jointly reviewed and action agreed.

The practical realities - endless, complex, demanding as they were - existed within a rich context of relationships: with doctors, nurses, friends, family and between the two of us.

There was no time at which we ever felt any kind of isolation; indeed there was such a constant outpouring of affection and support from professionals and friends alike that we were buoyed up by it in our storm-tossed sea which could otherwise have been so terrifying and threatening.

Between us there was a degree of peace and intimacy which intensified as the months progressed. We had, over the two years of illness, covered so much ground together - said all that we had to say, looked in the face of death, mourned the progressive loss of strength, faculty, our joint future - that we had nothing to do but be together, to relish each other's simple continuing existence. This, too, was part of his experience of quality.

We took leave of him at an emotional and extravagant funeral at the London Lighthouse; we had discussed it with the friend who was to be master of ceremonies on the day, and we knew it was to be a party. 'A leave-taking and a celebration of his life and courage' - with music chosen by him, with family and friends sharing their memories of him with tears, much laughter - and an inordinate amount of champagne.

It was a moving and wonderful occasion - with time and opportunity for companionable grief before and after the non-religious ceremony; with those who had had so much pleasure in his company leaning with their champagne on his coffin, as if it were a bar, talking, reminiscing, laughing, crying.

For me, it created such a vivid, rich picture of his thirty-two years that I felt him restored to me in his full vigour - moving the diminished, suffering patient into a less overwhelming perspective, placing it in the context of a whole life, full of energy, humour and pleasure. It was a grand finale which, to my surprise, left me strengthened and comforted, with a sense of fulfilment rather than bereavement.

I have felt, too, that my burden of grief has been less than I expected: we cried and mourned together a good deal over the last two years.

So, the house is empty, and I, bereft of the centre and anchor of my life. But he is still here, within me not in any bizarre psychic sense – but inasmuch as the fruits of living, sharing, learning, growing in the sweetness of intimacy can never be taken away.

Being single again is a miserable fact of life in the short term, but I face it with an enduring sense of fulfilment, of pride in what we made together of the hazardous enterprise of being human; and - like him - I face the future with a determination to find quality, not in idle aching for the unattainable, but in the best that is possible now, at this very moment."

## Grief Is Good

Grief is nature's way of getting us through this terrible time. Grief itself is not pain, it is merely a channel through which pain can be discharged. It is natural to grieve and process should not be resisted or circumvented.

When I worked on the problem page of a woman's magazine we had many letters from bereaved people who felt they were abnormal or that they were going mad because the grieving process was going on for "too long". After three months they were still crying, losing sleep, unable to eat properly, deeply depressed and still unable to accept that they would never see their loved one again. So many of them seemed to think it was morbid for their emotions to be in such turmoil. In fact it is natural and good still to be grieving deeply, even after a year in some cases.

The immediate reaction following bereavement will probably be one of numbness and disbelief. Your feelings may go on 'hold' for a while, but as they return you may become angry at the person who has died: "How could you do this to me?" you might ask. You may feel guilty that you didn't always behave as well as you could have done with your partner, or you may imagine that you treated him badly or didn't love him enough. In most instances, grief will do its job well and the guilt, anger, sadness, loneliness and incomprehension will subside into acceptance. Unfortunately there is no way that this process can be hurried, no way that the terrible pain can be avoided. However, bit by bit it lessens, little by little other emotions intrude. One day you might laugh, only to feel guilty and disloyal for being able to enjoy life again, even though your lover is dead. One day the early morning sunshine might lift your spirit, as it did all that time ago when you were two, and you will be slightly resentful that he can't be there to share it with you. But these little signals are telling you that the process of recovery has begun.

Talking to your friends and family about your loved one will help ease the sense of loss. If they are sensitive and understanding they will listen as you talk at great length and with apparent unflagging enthusiasm for the minutiae of the life you shared with your lover. Hopefully they will encourage you to talk and talk for as long as you wish, for such talking has a healing effect. If you see a bereavement counsellor it is likely that he or she will serve that purpose, too, encouraging you to talk endlessly about your lover and about your bewilderment at having lost him.

Eventually—and there is no 'right' period of time for this—you will be ready to pick up the threads of life again. What you must try to resist is the urge to escape the loneliness and heartache by seeking out another relationship before you have properly grieved for the last one. At such times your motives for entering this fresh relationship might not be what your new partner thinks they are. Are you really taking on this new partner because you feel he is the right person for you at this time in your life, or are you using him to escape the isolation and grief? Will you be able to judge this new man in his own right, bringing to your relationship his own special qualities, or are you seeking to replace a dead lover with a substitute? If you feel that somehow you can continue your lost relationship with a stand-in, you are heading for disillusion.

If you have met someone who you feel might be the one for you, then take your time. Explain your circumstances, that you want to avoid the pitfalls of rushing headlong into a new relationship for the wrong reasons, and ask him to be patient. You might enjoy each other's company, sex or a thousand other things, but reserve that final commitment until you are sure you are doing it for each other. At this stage it would be risky to make any large-scale practical changes in your circumstances - like giving up your accommodation.

There are practical problems associated with bereavement; elsewhere in this book I have encouraged you to consider the importance of sorting out your finances while both of you are capable. Bruce Hugman did all the right things, and his experiences provides an excellent object lesson. The minimum that needs to be done is a properly written will; it can save much heartbreak and ensure your lover gets what you want him to have. It is not unknown for families to make claims on a dead persons' estate to the exclusion of his gay lover. If there is no will making your wishes clear, your lover might end up not only lonely but homeless, too. At present the rules state that if an unmarried man or woman dies intestate (without making a will), the property is divided between his or her children or, if none, parents or, if they are dead, between his brothers or sisters. Wills take only a few hours to arrange, but can save months of anguish.

Your funeral arrangements should also be worked out in advance; if you feel strongly, for instance, that you lover should make the arrangements and not your family, make sure that it is made plain in writing. There have been tragic cases of the family moving in to take over the arrangements after the death of a gay man and excluding his lover from the funeral and other ceremonies. If you feel strongly that you want a specific kind of funeral (a certain religious ceremony or particularly a secular send-off) make sure that is clear too. Such things may seem morbid to contemplate when you are loving life, but in fact they express a desire to spare your lover extra misery should you die before him. The power of attorney, as described by Bruce Hugman, is also something that should be considered.

The Gay Bereavement Project has specially trained counsellors who will help you through the difficult times following bereavement (see contact list at the end of this book), and there are many books about coping with grief. Visit your library and read some of them, I am sure you will be comforted.

Your chances of making a fresh and successful start will depend on your circumstances. If you are elderly, or even middle-aged, you might be lucky enough to have a circle of supportive friends who will provide you with social outlets. However, finding a new partner might present you with problems. These difficulties are not unique to gay people, of course, although it has to be said that there are fewer obvious opportunities for older gays to socialise - the gay scene often seems to be dominated by discos and noisy pubs full of young people. But there are other outlets. Most non-commercial gay groups welcome people of all ages, and there is nothing to stop you becoming involved or even volunteering for some other organisation, such as

239

Switchboard or a political pressure group. Often the skills and experience of older gay people are undervalued in our youth-oriented culture, and it is time that we made more use of them. Getting involved in such voluntary activities will bring you into contact with a wide range of other gay people. At least by moving among your fellow gays there is always a possibility—however remote you might think it to be—that you might meet someone with whom you'd like to try again.

It is at times like these that the value of not allowing your relationship to be the sole focus of your social life will become clear. Having mutual friends is fine, but having your own friends is good too. Especially when you find yourself out on a limb.

# EPILOGUE

Now that you've read this book I hope that you'll agree that not only are gay relationships possible, they're frequently downright wonderful. But they don't get wonderful by themselves: they take work, sensitivity and constant vigilance in order to recognise the danger points.

However hard we strive, very few of us manage to reach the ideal. For every gay couple who takes the risk of committing to each other there are many developments that can't be anticipated or provided for. Sometimes you'll come upon events that are unique to your circumstances and there will be no ready-made answers. At times like that—and at most other times if we're honest—you'll have to employ creative thinking and make the rules up for yourself. Hopefully some of the advice in this book will help you lay the foundation to make such innovation easier. If both of you are determined to make your relationship work, then it will usually be possible to find amicable solutions to problems.

Human relationships are intensely complicated and difficult to maintain. If we imagine we are going to have a conflict-free relationship, we are heading for a big disappointment - or a life of unutterable boredom. Conflict is an essential element for sorting out differences, for confronting problems and for keeping the relationship growing. It shouldn't be avoided. We're all human and from time to time we will lose our temper, fly off the handle and there will be stand up rows and acrimonious arguments. Don't worry about this too much. So long as you have a mechanism for sorting out the differences when the dust settles, then all should be well. Anger that isn't openly expressed is likely to go underground, causing partners to undermine each other in other ways. If it is bottled up it may cause depression or might be expressed in an explosion of frustration - shouting, screaming, throwing things or physical attacks. A stand-up fight might get the issues on the table, but it won't sort them out. Eventually you'll have to face them rationally or else go on to another hurtful—and ultimately fruitless—battle.

We can be reassured by the fact that gay relationships have a number of inbuilt advantages - some of which are:

**1**. *Better communication*. After much research among homosexual couples, the sexologists Masters and Johnson wrote: "One can speculate that the uniquely high levels of communicative interchange characteristic of the homosexual couple may be the inevitable result of the partners' mutual effort to build their relationship into a strong bulwark. The research team had no other ready explanation for the consistently effective communicative interchange that was evidenced by committed homosexual partners and—with but a few outstanding exceptions—was comparatively absent in the married couples who participated."

**2**. *More honesty*. In an article in *Psychology Today* in 1975 ("Far from Illness: homosexuals may be healthier than straights") Mr Freeman wrote: "The social arrangements that prepare the way for a homosexual experience are often much more straightforward than in heterosexual situations...Gay people don't have to feign love or any other emotion...Many gays have a fairly complex understanding of self-disclosure, both in themselves and in others.

Moreover they are often more candid and open than non-gays." Other researchers, too, have found that gay couples tend to be less inclined to bottle up their emotions. While gay men generally are conditioned not to express their feelings, it has been shown that two men living together in a romantic relationship rapidly become skilled at saying how they feel.

**3**. *Lesser importance of power-structures*. As we've already discovered, gay relationships are very rarely modelled on straight marriages. More often male couples are likely to resemble romantically attached best friends, allowing their relationship to be more equal in power. Gay men in partnership become very good at adapting themselves to the jobs that need to be done and the roles that have to be taken in order to make their partnership function. "Gender role fluidity" has been noted, and it means that gay men are more willing to occasionally undertake the functions more usually associated with women, whether it is cleaning the house, cooking or being the 'receptive' partner in intercourse. It is only in rare instances that strict butch and femme roles are adopted – the disadvantages of such a set up are only too apparent.

**4**. *Gay couples are likely to be more affluent*. Readership surveys in gay magazines and newspapers repeatedly confirm what most had suspected: gay men are generally better off than their straight counterparts. If they are living in a relationship, it is likely that both partners are bringing in money—quite often relatively large amounts. They do not generally have the responsibility of children so their disposable income is substantial. The power of the 'pink pound' has not gone unnoticed by the commercial world and more and more big companies are targeting their products at the homosexual market. This affluence does not, of course, apply to all gay people. There are those who, for all kinds of reasons, are unable to earn money. However, the affluence odds are stacked in your favour.

**5**. *There are no pre-formed expectations*. There are no marriage contracts laying down the rules of our relationships as there are for straights. We can make it up as we go along. If we want to be monogamous, we can be. If we want to live in an 'open' relationship (and it's apparent from research that most of us eventually do), that's OK, too. There are no preachers, no teachers and no authorities to tell us that we are 'breaking tradition' if we live in a way that suits us best.

**6**. *No children*. For some people this is a cause for regret, but for most it means that life can be lived to the full. An article on 'Happiness' in *The Sunday Correspondent* (25 March, 1990) said that: "Survey after survey reveal that happiness levels begin to fall after the birth of a child, reaching the nadir in the teenage years and only returning to previous levels when the children leave home".

For those gay men who want to bring up children, there are few options. Adopting and fostering has become much more difficult for gay men, but some local authorities and agencies will still consider single men if they are appropriate. If you would like to pursue this, contact Lesbian and Gay Foster and Adoptive Parents Network, who might be able to supply some information. They can be contacted by post c/o London Friend (see listings).

From these advantages we can create a way of living which truly fits us like a glove. Even so, our imperfection as human beings also means that however alert we are to the pitfalls, we'll still stumble into some of them. Over an extended period there will be moments when temptation presents itself and isn't resisted (however much we warn ourselves about the possibly disastrous consequences), lies will be told, feelings hurt, thoughtless actions taken. We'll still try to manipulate from time to time or use power-plays in some area of life to get what we want from our partner. We'll lose our temper and shout and rant. That's OK - we're only human and we can but try. Hopefully these failings will be infrequent, and the ability to recognise them and say sorry at the appropriate times will help heal.

Your relationship can survive as long as you both want it to, you just need to let go of the myth that gay relationships don't last and, at the same time, embrace the truth that it is only hard work and commitment that makes them succeed. Your partnership can bring you intense joy, boundless love and the opportunity to explore the world with someone you regard as very special. And even if it doesn't last a lifetime, it can still have immense value.

Experiencing intense love feelings for someone doesn't guarantee that those feelings will be constant, and even the closest partnership will occasionally fall into the doldrums. There will be periods in your life together when you just don't feel particularly close, maybe because there are other calls on your time and energy which are temporarily draining you. A sudden upsurge in your career might mean that you must, for a while, shift the emphasis from your partner to your job. Hopefully your partner will understand this and be patient. Sometimes there doesn't seem to be any discernible reason why we don't feel close to our partner.

## Making Gay Relationships Work

We don't have to explain everything, sometimes we just have to accept.

But perhaps the most important thing of all is to take risks. Your efforts at loving someone may end in pain and disillusion but, then again, they're just as likely to provide long periods of pleasure and happiness. You won't know which it will be until you take the gamble. Holding back because you are afraid of potential hurt will simply ensure your life remains static and without incident. The American psychologist, Paul Hauck, wrote: "The life that has no risk in it is not worth living" - if you don't take the risks, you don't get the rewards. If you don't get it right the first time, keep on trying. Don't give up at the first or second or fifth hurdle - as long as you're both determined, you'll clear them all and go on to ever greater heights of happiness.

Most gay people have a few abortive attempts at making a relationship work before they get it right and although this may be painful, it does have its advantages. Each failed partnership will tell you something about yourself, and your hard-won experience will help you survive when you eventually find the man you really want to make a life with. A broken love affair might feel like a tragedy at first—and yes, it's OK to play your Shirley Bassey records and sob quietly into the pillow—but it will later be recognised as a useful learning experience, standing you in good stead for the next attempt.

Reading this book might have set established couples thinking about the structure and functioning of their existing relationship. Such couples should remember that what is written here is meant only as a guide, not as dogma set in concrete. There is no single volume that could tell you everything you need to know in order to succeed in sharing your life with another human being. We are all unique products of our personal history; our greatest task in life is to avoid becoming victims of that history, doomed to make the same mistakes over and over again.

If you have found your own successful way of loving that seems different to the ones I have described, then that is laudable. If you have worked out your own methods of settling differences, then good for you. If everything is fine, and both of you are content, don't be tempted to analyse your relationship to death; 'relationship fatigue' is a common problem for gay men who try to explain everything. As with a flourishing plant, if you keep pulling it out of the soil to see how the roots are doing, you risk causing severe damage.

Maybe not everyone in the world approves of your partnership, but that doesn't matter. There are enough people around who will love you and accept your relationship on its own terms. Seek those people out and create your own world of mutual respect and support. If you are happy then that is good news. If you are hopeful, I wish you every success.

Good luck, and good love!

# CONTACT LIST

There are many gay groups, support agencies and commercial operations around the country, so this list is far from exhaustive. However, as a useful starting point it includes places with a central pool of information. It's almost inevitable that this list will be out of date as soon as it is published - some groups fold, some move to new accommodation. You can find the latest listings in *Gay Times*. Telephone numbers contain a '1' as the second digit which should be omitted before September 1994.

**Aids Bereavement Support**
Tel: 01602-620920
24 hour helpline

**Albany Trust**
SUNRA Centre, 26 Balham Hill, London SW12 9EB
Tel: 0181-675 6669
Relationship & Psycho-sexual counselling,

**Gay and Lesbian Humanist Association**
34 Spring Lane, Kenilworth, Warks CV8 2HB
Tel: 01926-58450
Provides information about affirmation ceremonies without religion.

**Gay Times**
Ground Floor, Worldwide House, 116-134 Bayham Street,
London NW1 0BA
Tel: 0171-267 0021
National magazine available from some newsagents or on
subscription from the above address. Carries extensive news
reports as well as features and comprehensive listings.

**Lesbian and Gay Alcohol Problem Service**
34 Electric Lane, Brixton, London SW9
Tel: 0171-737 3579

**Lesbian and Gay Bereavement Project**
Vaughan M. Williams Centre, Colindale Hospital, London
NW9 5HG
Tel: 0181-455 8894
Provides counselling and practical support for those gay
people whose partner has died. Recorded message gives
name and telephone number of volunteer on duty that
evening from 7pm to midnight.

**Lesbian and Gay Christian Movement**
Oxford House, Derbyshire Street, Bethnal Green, London
E2 6HG
Tel: 0171-739 1249
Can provide information about blessing ceremonies.

**Lesbian & Gay Foster and Adoptive Parents Network**
By post c/o London Friend, see below

*Making Gay Relationships Work*

**London Friend**
86 Caledonian Road London N1 9DN (fully accessible)
Tel: 0171-837 3337 or 0171-837 2782. Minicom on both lines.
Various social and support groups (including ethnic, coming out and bisexual) operate from here.

**London Lesbian and Gay Switchboard**
Tel: 0171-837 7324
A twenty-four hour information and counselling line. It has a vast store of information and will attempt to help you with any problem related to your homosexuality. If it can't help directly, it can refer you on to a suitable agency that can. Lines often busy, keep trying.

**PACE** (Project for Advice, Counselling and Education)
2 Shelburne Road, London N7 6DL
Can provide counselling and advice for gay individuals and couples.
Tel: 0171-700 1323